Social Media Marketing and Personal Branding
2 books in 1
Build Your personal Brand And Learn the Best Marketing Advertising Online in 2020.
By: Gary Clarke

Social Media Marketing

Instagram, Facebook, Youtube, and Twitter Advertising Guide for Influencers in 2019 Through 2020
By: Gary Clarke

Table of Contents

Chapter 1

    1.0 Determining The Best Direction To Take
    1.1 How to Choose The Right Platform
    1.2 Learning About Your Customers
    1.5 Addressing Your Industry Influence

Chapter 2

    Linkedin
    2.0 Introduction
    2.1 Setting Up Shop on LinkedIn
    2.2 What's in the premium subscription?
    2.3 Creating a new LinkedIn profile
    2.4 Preparing a Content Strategy
    2.5 Covering What Matters First
    2.6.1 Finding connections
    2.6.2 Choosing to Advertise
    2.6.3 Participating in LinkedIn Groups
    2.6.4 Benefits of Joining Groups
    2.6.5 Starting your own group
    2.6.6 Leading a successful group
    2.6.7 Using LinkedIn to answer questions
    2.6.8 Finding A Job

Chapter 3

    Facebook
    3.0 Introduction
    3.1 Looking at Facebook Basics
    3.2 Starting With Search
    3.3 Facebook Pages

3.4 Facebook Groups
3.5 Facebook Events
3.6 Facebook Applications
3.7 Facebook Connect/Login with Facebook
3.8 The Use of Ads on Facebook

Chapter 4

Twitter
4.0 Introduction
4.1 Figuring Out Twitter
4.2 A Twitter handle
4.3 Preparing for Twitter Marketing
4.3.1 Twitter searches
4.3.2 Responding to tweets
4.3.3 Following and followers
4.3.4 Marketing via Twitter
4.3.5 Promoted accounts on Twitter
4.3.6 Making use of promoted tweets
4.3.7 Using promoted trends
4.3.8 Working with sponsored tweets
4.4 Tips and tricks

Chapter 5

Instagram
5.0 Introduction
5.1 Instagram for The Uninitiated
5.1.1 Signing up
5.1.2 Exploring the app
5.1.3 Using filters
5.1.4 Getting Found on Instagram
5.1.5 Structuring Instagram for Business Goals

5.1.6 Creating Content For Your Business
5.1.7 Curating and Sharing
5.2 Instagram stories
5.2.1 Instagram highlights
5.2.2 IGTV

Chapter 6

YouTube
6.0 Introduction
6.2 Why Social Media Marketing on YouTube?
6.3 Getting People to Subscribe to Your Channel
6.4 Promoting on YouTube
6.5 Modify your YouTube content
6.6 Tag and categorize everything you upload
6.7 Make response videos
6.8 Include a call to action
6.9 Important Note: Have fun, too!
6.10 Creating a Viral Campaign

Chapter 7

Pinterest
7.0 Introduction
7.1 Recognizing Pinterest Users
7.2 Exploring the Interests of Users
7.3 Pinning As A Social Activity
7.4 Becoming a Business Pinner
7.4.1 Setting up your profile
7.4.2 Example profile: Martha Stewart (MS)
7.4.3 Example profile: LL Bean
7.4.4 Starting a group board
7.4.5 Creating secret boards

7.5 Developing credibility for your profile
7.6 Narrowing down with guided search
7.7 Tracking your results

Chapter 8

Tumblr
8.0 Introduction
8.2 Setting Up Shop on Tumblr
8.2.1 Creating an account
8.2.2 Creating the good stuff
8.2.3 Finding and sharing the good stuff
8.3 Understanding your Tumblr activity

Chapter 9

Google+
9.0 Introduction
9.1 Looking at Google's Social Strategy
9.2 Grasping the Google+ Fundamentals
9.3 Google Brand Pages
9.4 Tips and Tricks For Google+
9.5 Learning from the examples of others
9.6 Listening to Google and Music

Conclusion

Chapter 1

1.0 Determining The Best Direction To Take

You may or may not be aware that the most popular social media platforms in this day and age were not the first to exist on the internet. Even the ones that we are dealing with in this book aren't the oldest. In fact, many platforms that came out before Facebook, Instagram, or Twitter and were equally successful in those eras. For example, SixDegrees.com launched in 1997 and has been considered the first social media website to be created. In the 90s, instant messaging became a fad and blogging started to gain traction as well.

However, social media is indeed a fickle thing. SixDegrees.com became defunct in 2001, only 4 years after it launched. Vine, a popular short video sharing app, was acquired and launched by Twitter in 2013 - only to shut down in 2016. Some platforms get bought out by bigger companies, forcing changes to be enforced (like when Facebook bought Instagram, or Microsoft bought Skype).

The point here is, change will always occur when it comes to social media. For the most part, there is a huge growth as people's curiosities are piqued and everyone wants to give it a try. And then the popularity plateaus as interest wanes and some customers decide that a particular website isn't really up their alley. In some cases, there's then a slow decline.

This definitely makes it difficult for marketers to reach their customers in the best way possible for them. How do you plan your campaign and budget when you have no idea whether this social media platform will still be active over the next few years? How do you keep up with the changes and ongoing trends in the current platforms? Having this kind of foresight is a rare thing in marketing. Nevertheless, you must try to answer those questions if you really want to up your game in reaching potential customers.

Before you even think about marketing on any social media platform, you need to figure out your social voice. This chapter aims to help guide you on where to start in determining the right combination of social platforms on which to launch, sustain, and promote your brand. If you are ready, here we go!

1.1 How to Choose The Right Platform

First of all, you need to understand that as a marketer, you cannot and should not limit yourself to using only one platform. That's the biggest marketing faux pas! You will not be able to maximize your reach with a single platform, as not all your customers use the exact same ones - nor do they use only one. Your customers will have at least two social media profiles and you must ensure you reach them on as many as possible. Furthermore, you have to assume that your consumers will invariably gravitate from one social platform to another as time passes. For example, whereas Facebook may have the greatest scale, the sharp rise in usage of Instagram, Pinterest, Tumblr, and WhatsApp shows how fickle consumers can be.

Additionally, you'll notice that it doesn't cost that much more to market on more than one social media platform. What is important is for you to have a clear focus and strategy across your entire marketing campaign - even if the execution is different for each platform. Using more than one undoubtedly makes sense if doing so allows you to reach a different demographic in different ways at different points in the marketing funnel.

You're probably still wondering where you should then focus your efforts. Given the vast number of platforms out there, it's not really possible (or advisable) to market all of them. Trying to do so may negatively impact your efforts as you may end up neglecting and that will look bad for your brand. Though it may be cheap, you're still going to have to expend time and money to maintain dozens of social media accounts. This can also come with some confusion and dissatisfaction to customers.

The solution here is to focus your marketing efforts on just the few that you know your customers use the most. Then you can have a lighter presence on others that you think might supplement your main marketing campaign.

To start off picking the right platforms to use, you need to take a closer look at your audience. See how you can interact with them and where they are making their purchasing decisions related to your company. For purposes of this discussion, you can break your audience down into the following three groups:

> 1. **Customers**: Obviously, this is your main target. You want to connect, interact, and prompt them to buy from you. You need to understand why they buy, where they buy, and what influences their purchasing process.

> 2. **Industry**: These are the people who may be competitors, vendors, governing bodies, and so on. In the social media world, this group helps to support your visibility and influence with media outlets and customers directly, too.

> 3. **Employees**: They can be either your greatest strength or weakness, depending on how you prepare them to participate in social media. If you don't have staff to dedicate to a project, you have a different kind of problem to solve.

Below is a look at how to work through the issues of picking platforms that support each group.

1.2 Learning About Your Customers

Choose where to practice social media marketing by researching and understanding where your customers are spending most of their time. This does not mean identifying where most of your customers have registered profiles, but instead researching where the customers have the highest levels of engagement. This means the following:

> • *Finding out what amount of time they spend on the social platform, what they specifically do, and how they use it to interact with other people.*

Tools like Quantcast (www.quantcast.com) can help you understand engagement, but you may need to reach out to the social platforms themselves to understand the details of the engagement. Keep in mind that with Quantcast, only if the site has been Quantified (which means that the site owner has added Quantcast code to his site) are the statistics the most accurate. comScore (www.comscore.com[1]), on the other hand, is a paid solution that can provide more accurate numbers for non-Quantified sites.

You may also want take a survey of your customers directly to understand their social media usage. There are several good survey tools, including SurveyMonkey (https://www.surveymonkey.com/) and Zoho Survey (https://www.zoho.com/survey/).

> • *Understanding the user behaviors on the social platform.*

For example, let's say that you're a business-to-business (B2B) solutions provider. You see that your customers use LinkedIn to ask each other for advice when making business-related purchasing decisions but spend a lot more time on Facebook. In this case, LinkedIn may still be a better place to practice social media marketing since that's where

---

1. http://www.comscore.com

they are making the purchasing decisions that matter to you. It doesn't matter if they're spending more cumulative minutes on Facebook.

In addition, consider monitoring mentions of your brand, competitors, product names, or industry keywords to determine how much activity occurs across the platforms.

Invariably, you discover that three to four social platforms match your customers' demographics, have high engagement levels for them, and are what we loosely call locations of influence as far as your product category is concerned. That's where your customers make their decisions, get influenced by others, and observe how their peers are purchasing or discussing their own purchases. These factors together tell you where to practice social media marketing. And as you do so, recognize that you must also consider two broader aspects:

> 1) **Watching the macro trends of the social platform.** For example, is the platform an emerging one, has it settled into a plateau, or is it fizzling? Accordingly, you may want to devote more or fewer dollars and effort to it.

> 2) **Determining whether the social platform is a place where your brand will have permission to participate and one in which you will want to participate.** Participating in some social platforms may hurt your brand. For example if you are a high end, exclusive brand like Chanel, it may not be appropriate to engage in conversations in a casual, music-oriented social environment like the new version of Myspace.

Your customers move between platforms as time passes. As a result, be prepared to adjust your social media marketing campaign significantly. Your customers may not always stay on the platforms that you're targeting currently. This potential migration matters especially to small business marketers.

Each social network has a reputation. Make sure that your brand is in alignment with that reputation. For example, Tumblr is known to be photocentric and has a reputation for attracting a young, creative user. Keep a platform's reputation in mind as you choose where and how to market.

1.5 Addressing Your Industry Influence

A look at your industry yields a very long list of potential competitors, partners, vendors, and associations for you to connect with. The social media marketing goal is to make this group aware of your influence in the marketplace. There are a lot of tools around social media that are available for your use. With this tools, you can compile and gather information, such as the following:

SOCIAL MENTION (http://socialmention.com/) is a free to access service that allows users to search for information just about anything. All that is required of you is for you to type in the name of your company and it searches over a hundred social media properties to streamline all the information you would need. This includes strength, sentiment, and reach. It even gives you general keywords surrounding your search term.

MARKETING GRADER (https://website.grader.com/) evaluates the marketing on your website using Hubspot's tool for grading websites. It looks at a variety of measures, including your traffic rank, indexed pages, and linking domains.

FOLLOWERWONK (followerwonk.com) can evaluate your Twitter account and provide a visual depiction of your Twitter feed according to influence, popularity, engagement, and user habits.

You now have a basic idea of what it takes to determine how to best go about social media marketing. It's certainly no walk in the park but if done properly and with due diligence, it should yield the best results possible for your brand. Just remember that it's not about dipping your toes into all the platforms out there! Know your audience and focus your energies on those that work best for them because in the ends, that's also what'll work best for you.

The next few chapters you are about to read will dive deeper into a few of the more popular social media platforms in the industry today. The chapters will also explain how you can utilize these platforms to build your social media marketing campaigns.

Chapter 2

Linkedin

2.0 Introduction

Many years ago, interacting with people was so limited to a specific region and communicating overseas can be a bit of a tremendous job and unlikely to catch the interest of many. Thankfully, when the web was invented, everything became possible as people can now socialize with others abroad by just using their devices every time and anywhere across the globe! You can get to know people that are also connected with your peers.

Linkedin is a little different from other social media platforms that we know like Instagram, Twitter, or Facebook because it focus on the corporate world. It provides details about your most recent or new workplace or new shopping acquisition among many others. The tone is serious and the social media marketing potential is vast because people join the platform to network. If you sell to a business audience of any kind, LinkedIn can provide you with a great focus group of interested members. According to a study done by BtoB magazine in April 2011, 26 percent of B2B marketers cite LinkedIn as their single most important social channel, with 20 percent choosing Facebook, 19 percent citing blogging, and 14 percent citing customer communities.

When LinkedIn (www.linkedin.com) launched in May 2003, many questioned whether it truly fit the mold of a social media networking site. LinkedIn has grown from having 79 million users in March 2011 to 300 million in May 2014. That's tremendous growth!

Why did LinkedIn grow so robustly? Like all the other popular social networks, it met a need. It provided a way for like-minded business people from around the globe to find each other, share information, and give advice. It legitimized a way for professionals to communicate in an environment that had guidelines and accountability.

The key to success is remembering that LinkedIn is just one channel of your social media strategy. You need to pay attention to how your connections here can drive traffic to other social media platforms. For example, you may want to provide a link to a discount on your website. By integrating selling with everything else you're doing, you won't seem like a crass self-promoter.

In this chapter, we look at LinkedIn's varied uses for social marketing of both yourself and your company, starting off with the basics: how to get started? From there, we'll talk about how you can use the strong profile you've built to expand your network using the LinkedIn groups. As a bonus, the latter part of the chapter covers how you can market yourself *as an individual*.

2.1 Setting Up Shop on LinkedIn

You can look at the marketing potential of LinkedIn in two ways: First, as a tool to help out your own career as an individual. Second, as a tool to understand your audience better in order to interact with and market to them more appropriately as a company.

Considering the way LinkedIn is structured, you can assume that everyone on it is open to the idea of networking. After all, LinkedIn is primarily for networking and the members understand that any connection made on the website is valuable. However, this also means that you can't be too frivolous when making connections on LinkedIn. At no time should you connect with someone without the understanding that you or your contacts could also be of value to them.

Going back to getting started, LinkedIn gives you the option to start with a free account which you can always upgrade later on if you feel the need to do so. The free account already has tons of free features, so you can use this to explore and get a feel of the platform first. If you decide later on that it'll be worth it to make a financial commitment, then you're welcome to upgrade your account.

If you've already been using LinkedIn and want to get started on using it to build your brand right away, then jump right into LinkedIn Premium.

2.2 What's in the premium subscription?

A few of the most useful features are:

InMail: This premium feature allows you to email anyone on LinkedIn regardless of whether that person is in your network or not, although you are restricted to a certain number of emails. A free account lets you access only your immediate network. Note: If you do not get a response from the person to whom you sent the email, that user is not counted toward your monthly limit. The Business premium account allows three InMails per month; the Business Plus premium account allows 10 InMails per month; the Executive premium account allows 25 InMails per month.

More access to profiles and people when you search: A premium account allows you to see more profiles than you would if you have a free account. This access to more profiles increases the likelihood that you will find the right person to connect with.

Search filters: You can apply a variety of filters to your search so that you can zero in on the right target. For example, you can search for people who work for a certain size company or target only the Fortune 1000.

Expanded profiles: When you see profiles, you see a more expanded profile of the people in which you are interested. You also see everyone on LinkedIn who fits the criteria, not just those limited to your own network.

Who Viewed My Profile: This feature of the free account allows you to see who viewed your profile. The list is restricted to a few names and profiles. However, with a premium account, you can see *everyone* who is interested in you and how each person found you.

With all of these additional premium features, you're probably asking yourself: how much will all of this cost you? You have the following payment options[1]:

- Business: This is the first tier. If you choose to prepay for the annual subscription, it is $287.88 (at the rate of $23.99 per month). The monthly rate is $29.99.

- Business Plus: At this tier, you prepay $575.88 annually (at the rate of $47.99per month). The monthly rate is $59.99.

- Executive: At the highest tier, you prepay $899.88 annually (at the rate of $74.99 per month). The monthly rate is $99.99.

To see the number of users you can access using specific features at each tier, c the subscription chart on the LinkedIn website.

If you are more than a casual user of LinkedIn, you may want to try a premium account. The premium levels specifically for job seekers are discussed later in this chapter, in the section "Finding a Job."

2.3 Creating a new LinkedIn profile

Regardless of whether you're using it for personal career goals or consumer research, the general tone of any interaction will definitely be formal and professional. Therefore, you need to look over your general business strategy to see which of your goals can be propagated on LinkedIn.

After figuring that out, you need to move a step forward to finding out the best way to present yourself to your potential connections. To do this, you need to set up your profile. Now, you can only set up one profile so you need to make sure that it suits all of your needs.

You could opt to set up a company page from the outset, but we don't really advise that you do that right away. We recommend that you wait until you're more familiar with LinkedIn to do this - unless you're setting up a page with several employees already. It's just better to be able to navigate the platform expertly in case you make a mistake.

Setting up a LinkedIn profile is really easy - it just takes some work. It's better to spend more time on making an account so that you can give as many details as possible - quality is the most important part of your profile. Considering it's a professional activity, anyone who looks into you and your company will be judging you on a number of things, including previous achievements and successes, as well as your knowledge on specific subject matter.

We also recommend that you start building your profile around the main goals of your marketing campaign. After that, you revise it as you go along to support more details. For example, if you're looking for a job, your profile will have different content from that of a business owner doing market research. We cover these differences in the rest of the chapter.

2.4 Preparing a Content Strategy

You've probably heard a good deal about the concept of content strategy. It boils down to evaluating what content you have and what you need to meet a specific marketing goal. Content can be articles, product descriptions, videos, audio interviews, or any material that informs people about you or your business.

To illustrate, one of your LinkedIn goals might be to find new consulting clients. If this is the case, you want to review all the content you have created that shows off your consulting expertise. Then you can start to share it on your profile. Afterwards, you can use this newly repurposed content on other platforms, such as your newsletter or blog.

Begin by doing an inventory of your e-books, posts, proposals, and so on, and determine what content you can use to let colleagues learn about you on LinkedIn. Then make an editorial schedule for yourself so that you can create in a timely manner any new items you need. Usually if you don't schedule a specific time to do this, you may end up not doing it. For inspiration, look at other people's profiles and see what they have posted.

2.5 Covering What Matters First

Your profile continues to evolve as you meet new people, join more groups, and attend events. You can't do everything all at once. Consider the following tips when you are starting out:

1. **Keywords matter.**

We made keywords the focal point and first one on the list of what we are discussing. This is necessary because as you put together your profile, you will want to make sure that you include keywords that can be used to find you. You probably have some keywords that you already use for your websites and other channels. Make sure to include some of those, but also think through the goal of this profile and include any new keywords that will move you toward the top of the search results.

1. **List the professional name you wish to be known by.**

This is the name you use in your industry. You want colleagues and potential connections to find you. Don't use a nickname unless you use it professionally.

LinkedIn lets you create only one profile, so if you own a business, decide ahead of time whether you intend to use your own name or your business name. We recommend that you use your own name in case you close your business or want to change direction.

1. **Use a real headline, not just a title**.

This section introduces your brand. If someone were to give you a wonderful introduction, it would include this content. If you are a bestselling author or award-winning salesperson, or have some special designation, this is the right place to use it (for example: Jane Smith, Award-Winning Salesperson).

1. **Provide a summary that highlights your uniqueness**.

Here you detail the contents of your headline. Think of this as the follow-up to the headline. Imagine that you are speaking right after the person who introduced you. Explain who you are and what makes you different among a sea of other members. Don't be modest - the point here is to really sell and market yourself!

1. **Think carefully about how you list your positions — current and past**:

Display what you are doing now and any significant positions you previously held. This is not a detailed résumé. If you are seeking a new job, see the section later in this chapter called "Finding a Job."

1. **Supply a professional photo**.

This is a key item on LinkedIn. People don't like to admit it because they like to be able to picture the person with whom they're connecting. It's not a beauty contest. Get a professional photo with appropriate attire. Save the pose with your favorite pooch for Facebook.

1. **Use links other than just websites**.

Don't be too literal. You can put in any link that you want to send people to. It doesn't have to be your main website. Just make sure that any link you provide are relevant and polish your brand.

1. **Look at the ways in which you can list your achievements.**

The possible sections available include Education, Certifications, Patents, Languages, Honors and Awards, Organizations, Projects, and Publications and Test Scores. Use any of these that are pertinent. You have wide latitude here to really showcase your talents. Again, make sure you sell yourself.

1. **Ask for recommendations.**

LinkedIn provides a recommendations tool that you can use to solicit comments from people who you may have worked with in the past or present and have been impressed by you. This could include a coworker, manager, or client. Obviously, you want to have great recommendations but don't go crazy at the start. Perfunctory recommendations from your friends aren't all that valuable. If someone has some real value to add, ask for their recommendation when you get started. This section will grow organically because your colleagues want to commend you (and have you commend them) for a job well done.

To make it easier for other LinkedIn members to endorse you, make sure to add a list of skills that you want to highlight in the Skills section of your profile. When other members look at the list, they can pick from skills that you want them to endorse instead of inventing them.

1. **Start making connections.**

Connections are at the heart of LinkedIn's success. You are here to build your network. Remember that these connections are people who will help you reach your goals, so make them meaningful. Don't be in a race to see how many connections you can get. After you reach 500 connections, LinkedIn will only lists your connections as 500+. See more details in

"Finding Connections," later in this chapter.

1. **Show work samples.**

LinkedIn has added the ability for you to add your work samples to your profile. Content types include video, images, podcasts, and so on. You should take advantage of this feature when you get started. This way you can highlight your best work up front. You can add samples in the Summary, Education, and Experience sections. This function replaces the built-in app section.

2.6 Accessing LinkedIn from your mobile devices

Of course, you'll want to stay connected when you're on the go if you're searching for a job using LinkedIn. LinkedIn makes it easy to access your connections from your smartphones and mobile devices. You'll find free apps for the following:

- Iphone
- Ipad
- Blackberry
- Android
- Windows

2.6.1 Finding connections

LinkedIn helps you easily get started in finding new connections. One way to start is to click the Connections tab and then click Add Connections. You have several options to choose from. You can find colleagues from your various email programs such as Outlook, classmates from your educational institutions, or people you may know from nonprofits or clubs.

As you are presented with lists of these contacts, go through and choose the ones you want. Be certain to deselect the 'Share All' checkbox so that you do not send invitations to people who don't belong in your network but are on your email lists.

It's really that simple! Growing your professional network has probably never been this easy. You have now gotten your profile set up and have a good understanding of how LinkedIn works. Let's move on to how you can use this platform for your social media marketing campaigns and build your network.

2.6.2 Choosing to Advertise

In contrast to some other social media platforms, advertising on LinkedIn involves little controversy. Perhaps LinkedIn's business orientation keeps the idea of advertising from seeming intrusive. When you are on the site, you find ads on the following pages: Home, Profile, Inbox, Search Results, and Groups.

It's important to know who exactly you're targeting on LinkedIn because the platform makes it very easy for you to separate your ad targets. You can segment your audience into the following groups:

- **Industry:** You can choose a variety of industries applicable worldwide. On LinkedIn, Zoomsphere.com reports that the top five industries are Higher Education (18.7%), Information Technology and Services (13.9%), Financial Services (11.6%), Retail (10.9%), and Computer Software (8.9%).

- **Seniority:** This refers to job seniority, or a person's position in their company. 2 million users on LinkedIn identify themselves as members of C-suite jobs (i.e. jobs with a C in the title, like CEO, CTO, CFO, or COO).

- **Geography:** You can target your audience based on where they are either by region, continent, or country. The United

States makes up the largest demographic on LinkedIn with over 27% of users.

- **Job function:** These include Sales, Management, Business Development, Information Technology, and Marketing.

- **Age**: In the United States, 41 percent of the members are between the ages of 35 and 54.

As soon as you have a better understanding of your audience and customers, you can then determine which of the above subgroups you can target such that you get the best results from.

2.6.3 Participating in LinkedIn Groups

Many LinkedIn users don't fully understand the usefulness and value of joining or participating in groups. That's probably because they see the platform as only a medium to find or further their personal careers. People probably forget that it's possible to reach out to your connections' connections to expand your network for whatever reason you need. Joining a group on LinkedIn goes even further beyond that, as you can meet people that you really never would have met in person.

2.6.4 Benefits of Joining Groups

There are many ways that you can get started in LinkedIn groups. One strategy is to join several groups in order to gain as many contacts with similar interests as possible. Another is to simply join one, see how you like it, and then expand your groups from there. You are allowed to join a total of 50 groups, so you can always take your time to decide which of the groups will help you achieve your marketing goals.

Below are some benefits you can get from joining groups:

• **Finding members with similar experiences**. This can include people who work or worked in the same company, or went to the same school as you.

- **Expanding your knowledge of a company in which you are interested.** If you're thinking about working for or partnering with a particular company, you can find other employees to connect with.

- **Connecting with members who are interested in the same activities.** Nonprofit and charitable groups are in abundance. You can find like-minded members easily.

- **Establishing yourself as an expert in your field**: You can choose to take a leadership role in a group or make your feelings known about certain discussion topics.

- **Understanding the trends in your industry**: You can stay informed about important issues and developments.

- **Determining who the industry leaders are**: By virtue of their popularity and activities, you can learn from industry leaders who are active.

- **Connecting with and participating in discussions**: You can do a lot of consumer research in these groups if you take the time to read and listen.

- **Finding partners for joint venture activities**: If you're looking for investors, you may want to extend your feelers out in the group without having to give away too much information.

- **Discovering new clients**: People who are impressed with your breadth of knowledge on a topic can seek you out for consultation.

2.6.5 Starting your own group

If you have determined that starting your own group will better help you meet your business goals, you'll be happy to know that LinkedIn provides a great framework for you to do so. The most important thing to consider before starting is whether you have the time and enthusiasm to be the leader. Managing a group takes work. If you start a group and then let it falter, it reflects badly on your professionalism. With more than 300 million people as potential members, you can develop a solid group fairly quickly but it's your responsibility to keep it lively and active.

Imagine yourself as the host of a party that needs your attention to be a success. This is particularly true for small business owners who wear all the hats in their organization. Picture yourself running this group a year from now and see how that fits into your plans.

Rather than hope that everyone will police their own groups, LinkedIn has set some guidelines. They include the following:

1. **You can send only one email a week to members of your group.**

You can envision the amount of email that could be generated by a group leader eager to connect (and sell things) to his members. Limiting email communications helps everyone control the information flow and that's actually cool.

1. **The group must either be open or closed (by invitation only).**

You can choose to have an invitation-only group or an open one. If you choose a closed group, members must be approved by the group leader. The members so approved are the only ones who can see and participate in discussions.

If you choose to have an open group, anyone can join. You should be aware that the discussions generated in an open group can be seen by anyone on LinkedIn, not just group members. In addition, the content can be shared on Facebook and Twitter. Leaders of open groups can decide whether everyone on LinkedIn can participate in discussions or just be able to view them.

The group leader can allow members to invite people to join the group. As the group leader, you can allow members to seek out new members for the group by sending them invitations. If they accept an invitation from another member, they are instantly accepted.

2.6.6 Leading a successful group

What are the components of a highly-reputable group on Linkedin? You can build a successful business connection in this social media site. This is obviously what you can achieve by socializing with people effectively as part of a community. Below are the techniques that you can do for you to have a successful group in Linkedin:

1. **Use your weekly email**

You are allowed to send only one email a week, so make it count. Think of it as the newsletter you might send to your website mailing list. Provide value and help members discover each other.

1. **Hold the line on promotions**

As the leader, you are responsible for making sure that other members are not over-promoting and ruining the experience. Nothing is worse than feeling like you're being taken advantage of by other group members.

1. **Encourage discussions**

The discourse in the groups are a valuable part of your content - both for you and your consumers. You'll be able to understand your audience better based on what they know or don't know. On the other hand, your customers will gain more information based on other users' experience.

1. **Use events**

As I have said a while ago, LinkedIn has a very functional tool that can be used in events. You can produce several virtual events wherein members can interact with one another. You can get everyone active about upcoming events. If you have caught the attention of a lot of people then you can start an in-person conference.

1. **Catch the Attention of the Media**

One of the assignments you need to pursue for your group is to ensure that you gain visibility from the media. This is essential because a highly visible group will do a lot of wonders for your group to become popular. You can have an idea of producing an eBook or other digital products about your niche and give the privilege for the media to get a grasp of it.

2.6.7 Using LinkedIn to answer questions

For you to transform yourself into an outstanding leader on LinkedIn, it is really great to disseminate advice to people. The people who utilize LinkedIn put up some inquiries that needs some professional help. Letting others know your field of specialization is an excellent resort to give a function and it will eventually lead to people noticing you.

SOCIAL MEDIA MARKETING AND PERSONAL BRANDING

One of the greatest ways to give help is with the use of LinkedIn Answers, however, the feature is already not available as it was removed several months ago. Based on LinkedIn, the most effective resort to disseminate your specialization is by using the following features:

- Your LinkedIn Home page
- LinkedIn discussion groups
- Partner sites
- LinkedIn Pulse

LinkedIn Pulse is a news feed gathered by LinkedIn that can be accessed by going to Interests*Pulse in the main menu of your profile. Here you will find news based on your interests as determined by your LinkedIn preferences. In addition, you will see a link to Top Posts on the service and a 'Discover link' that displays suggested people you may want to follow.

Answering questions has an extra function to people that are marketing with the use of social media. For an instance, you can acquire the corresponding benefits:

- **Discovering content for blog posts, e-books, and slideshows**: The greatest resort to produce content is by answering queries. It will also enhance the content that people have are interested in and at the same time you can help a lot of people. If they are not clear to other people, then you can still use it to your advantage by making an additional post regarding it with the use of different media.

- **Uncovering trends by mining the questions people are asking**: If you have seen a latest innovation that is formed, you may have discovered the latest trend. Always be vigilant!

- **Searching for a prospect business partner**: If you are looking for an expert in a particular area, you can ask questions to find other thought leaders who may want to partner with you (or invest).

- **Finding a technical expert**: Locating a technical expert who you understand and trust can be a herculean task. If you find someone who answers your technical questions and can act as a freelancer or consultant, you have saved yourself a lot of time, energy, and money.

- **Letting new clients find you**: A great by-product of showing off your skills is that someone with a budget to buy your products or hire you could be listening. Be generous with your expertise and let people get to know you. They'll be more likely to consider working with you.

2.6.8 Finding A Job

It is now common to have a LinkedIn account if you are trying to look for a job. For basic use, there is no payment required and the good thing is that employers are always online to look for new people that they can hire. However, you must have an excellent-looking profile, build significant amount of contacts, and have fundamentals when it comes to different groups that are related with your niche. Below are tips for you to get noticed by employers:

1. **View your profile from the perspective of an employer**

Place yourself in the shoes of a business as you investigate your profile. On the off chance that a genuine list of qualifications style is required, you can look at Resume Builder at http://resume.linkedin-labs.com. This application encourages you to take your profile and fabricate a gorgeous resume from it, however LinkedIn likewise has a worked in highlight that enables you to transform your profile into a list of references. Survey it cautiously to ensure that the sequential request is precise and matches your profile. If you look for a structure work, ensure that you transfer PDFs, pictures, introductions, and any other thing you need to flaunt.

1. **Produce a compelling presentation**

Furthermore, if you create your résumé to make it appear excellent, ensure that it has great presentation.

Programs such as Prezi can be used to develop something unique. You can also link to SlideShare (http://www.slideshare.net) or post a video. It's worth repurposing your best work and showing it off. You need a way to stand out, and this will help.

1. **Reexamine your keywords**

You may have chosen general keywords when you first signed up. Now that you know specifically what type of job you are searching for, add keywords that will help you get found by your preferred employers.

1. **Create a list of companies you would like to work for**

Even if you are not targeting a specific company, making a list of potential companies will help you. Do some research on what jobs they have open and where you might fit in. It will give you ideas about how to improve your profile. If you do have a target list, look for someone in the company who you might be able to approach for discussion.

1. **Target your recommendations**

If you've been reticent about asking for recommendations, now is the time to actively seek out people whose endorsement speaks directly to the job you want. LinkedIn makes adding a recommendation easy, so it's not an onerous request.

1. **Mine your network**

Look at the second- and third-degree contacts in your network and see whether you want to ask for introductions. That's when the power of LinkedIn is really demonstrated. Get started immediately because this could take some time. Not everyone has the same sense of urgency that you do.

1. **Include other channel links**

Don't forget that there is a whole wide world of other online channels that you are connected to.

Make sure to showcase a website or show that you have an active Twitter following.

1. **Consider purchasing Job Seeker Premium services.**

LinkedIn provides special subscription premium tiers for job hunters. If you are considering this, you may want to start with a month-to-month subscription to see whether it works for you. If you find that the job hunt is slow, you can always move to an annual subscription. How much will you have to pay for premium job seeker services? You have the following payment options[2]:

- Job Seeker Basic: This is the first tier. If you choose to prepay for the annual subscription, it is $191.88 (or $15.99 per month). You pay $19.99 go from month to month.

SOCIAL MEDIA MARKETING AND PERSONAL BRANDING

- Job Seeker: At this tier, you prepay $287.88 annually (at the rate of $23.99 per month). You pay $29.99 to go from month to month.

Job Seeker Plus: At the highest tier, you prepay $575.88 (at the rate of $47.99 per month). You pay $59.99 to choose a monthly subscription.

A few of the most helpful features included in the premium accounts are as follows:

- **Job Seeker "Premium" Badge**: Your profile has a visual aid next to it. This helps employers quickly spot you. You can choose to display your badge (or not) in Settings, which is the pull-down menu you see when you click your name in the upper right of the home page. The default choice is Off.

- **See real salary information**: You can zero in on your desired level and see real details from employers.

- **InMail**: As mentioned previously in the section "Getting Started," depending on the premium level you choose, you can contact a set number of members directly.

- **Who's Viewed My Profile**: As we noted previously, this feature allows you to see who viewed your profile. With a premium account, you can see everyone who is interested in you and how anyone found you.

- **Job Seekers Group and Webinar**: Here you can get additional support and advice from the community to help you find a job.

The key to finding a job on LinkedIn is to work the power of your network. Not only can you find almost anyone in the industry or companies you target, but you can also market yourself in the best possible light. Remember that recruiters and employers use LinkedIn on a regular basis. If you make the effort, you could be in the right place at the right time.

Given all of this information about how to build a network both for yourself and your brand on LinkedIn, you should be able to jump on the platform with confidence. With LinkedIn, everything is viewed with more professionalism than what is obtainable on other social media platforms. These platforms will be discussed in the succeeding chapters.

Chapter 3

Facebook

3.0 Introduction

No matter which way you look at it, it's highly likely that Facebook will be a great platform that you can use at hand.

Facebook was founded in 2004 and up till this present moment, it has recorded a significant growth having more than 1 billion active users. It is the largest social network in the United States. Of all users with an account on Facebook, more than 48% log in every day.

Statista.com reports that approximately 201 million North Americans are active on Facebook monthly. Given this information, it's pretty safe to assume that a huge percentage of your customers are not only users of the platform, but are on it at any given time.

According to Facebook Chief Operating Officer Sheryl Sandberg, you should be "social by design." By that she means that social media marketing should be a part of everything you do. With this idea in mind, in this chapter we jump into explaining how you can develop marketing strategies. We also discuss how you can use Facebook to grow your audience and engage your customers through Pages, Events, and Ads.

3.1 Looking at Facebook Basics

Choosing how to use internet-based marketing on Facebook can appear to be threatening in light of the fact that so much is going on at one time. The profile page for every substance has a large group of connections, advertisements, posts, etc. Likewise, changes to the stage itself are being made ceaselessly. You may feel that when you see how something functions, it changes, and this can appear to be overpowering. One approach to conquer this feeling of feeling overpowered is to recall the accompanying:

- The gateway to web-based social networking promoting on Facebook is to comprehend that your system is the key.

Together, you and your companions do things online that may influence each other's conduct. Advertisers endeavor to tackle this movement to their very own favorable position. That is the thing that you have to concentrate on. For instance, if a few clients like your item, their companions will see that suggestion and maybe get it, as well. By understanding the interconnectedness of internet-based marketing, particularly on Facebook, you can construct your business.

- *The heart of Facebook is a user's Newsfeed.*

It is easy to forget that the heart of Facebook is not your Facebook page or a user's profile page. Rather, it is the Newsfeed. This is the page that a user sees immediately they log into Facebook. It shows their friends' activities (including potentially your brand's activity). In 2013, Facebook redesigned the newsfeed so that users would have an easier way to show their followers what matters most to them. Some users have complained that the algorithm that supports this redesign (called Edgerank) actually makes it harder for their fans to see their daily content.

Because it's now harder to predict what your users will see, focusing your Facebook marketing efforts on the Newsfeed is extremely important. A lot more users may learn about your company or your product through the Timeline rather than by visiting your particular company page.

- *Using Facebook requires constant experimentation.*

No one right way to market on Facebook exists. Your audience and products are unique. You can follow some best practices but for the most part, you have to determine what works for your specific audience. If you understand this idea going in, you won't have to feel as though you're failing because things are moving slowly at first. Try something and see how it works. Then use feedback and results to point you in the right direction.

- *You have powerful tools at your disposal to enhance all your other channels.*

Facebook gives you tools to link to other channels where you can promote your company or your products. For example, you can link to your blog, your Twitter account, and so on. Provide a link anywhere you have an opportunity. Don't forget to link all your email addresses and newsletters to your Facebook account as well. For example, when people are on your website, make sure that they see a widget for your Twitter account. Go to the link for "Take Twitter with you" at twitter.com to get the widget to link your Twitter account to your website and other social media platforms.

- *Facebook gives you an SEO (search engine optimization) advantage.*

The search engines regard Facebook Connect as very important content. By publishing to your Facebook page, you can see a potential boost in your rankings.

- *You can easily reach local customers.*

With Facebook, you can easily let customers know where you are, and you can choose to include a map. When customers are at your location, they can also choose to let their friends know. Furthermore, you can target specific posts on Facebook to certain customers only.

- *Pay attention to your Timeline.*

Your Timeline is the place where everyone goes to get your updates. Keep things lively! If you publish only once in a while, people are going to lose interest. Make it a point to put a process in place, and use content calendars to manage the frequency and types of postings to the Timeline.

- *The number of Likes you have should not be your only measure of success.*

The number of Likes you have is only one indicator of interest at a particular point in time. You may have lots of Likes and few engaged customers or buyers, or vice versa. Use several measures, including looking at Facebook's own Insights, to see how you are doing. Pay particular attention to Facebook's People Talking About metric. This represents how many people are interacting with you, such as Liking your page, posting on your Timeline, and commenting or sharing your content. You can find it in Facebook Insights.

Facebook is always in the process of evolving its social platform. Besides the guidance we give in the sections that follow, we recommend visiting Inside Facebook (www.insidefacebook.com) and All Facebook (www.allfacebook.com) to keep pace with the evolving marketing opportunities and advertisement formats on the platform.

3.2 Starting With Search

"In the beginning, there was Search." It will always be.

Okay, that's not *exactly* the right phrase, but just as you do with any good investigation into a subject, you may want to start with a search. When you are determining what's already on Facebook and how that relates to your own social media marketing plan, you want to use Facebook Search, which you can find at www.facebook com/search.

You can narrow your search by using the drop-down menu to select the following:

- All Results

- People
- Apps
- Events
- Web Results

By starting with a search, you can get a good understanding of what exists in your product or service category. For example, if your category is productivity, you can enter that search term and get the results. Then you can filter further by using one of the search categories, such as apps.

The idea is to get an understanding of your customers, competit0rs, and Facebook users' way of doing things. We recommend that whenever you want to investigate a question about the Facebook universe, start here.

3.3 Facebook Pages

Facebook has 30 million active small business pages and counting. Think of Facebook pages as company profiles on Facebook. You can set up a page for your brand and encourage others to "Like" it. It doesn't cost anything to create a business page, but it does take time and effort to make the page relevant and worthwhile.

Don't confuse a Facebook page with a personal profile. A personal profile has your name on it and is about you and your friends. A page is devoted to an entity such as a business, charity, or public figure.

The first thing you need to do is decide what type of page it will be. The choices include:

- Local Business or Place
- Company, Organization, or Institution
- Brand or Product
- Artist, Band, or Public Figure
- Entertainment
- Cause or Community

As you can see, you are provided with a variety of options for your business. Getting started should be easy.

After you've selected your category, you need to decide what to add to your page to help it garner attention. If you begin to think like a social media marketer, you want to consider publishing media that includes the following:

- **Posts, including location-based posts**: Ongoing posts that keep your community informed are necessities. Post as often as you can, but keep it relevant.

- **Photo albums**: You can easily add a set of photos to Facebook in the form of an album. You can add up to 200 photos per album and an unlimited number of albums. Make sure to add any pertinent photos of your products, services, staff members, and anything else that will inspire your customers.

- **Multimedia content**: To ensure that you provide a variety of formats, you can link to slides, videos, and podcasts. Remember that your audience likes to be surprised.

- **Twitter feeds and blog posts:** You can easily link your Twitter feed or blog to show up in your status updates using a plug-in. For example, to link your Twitter feed to Facebook, go to this URL: www.facebook.com/twitter/.

- **Event information**. The opportunity to alert your community to your events is priceless. You can also show the location with a map. See the section "Facebook events," later in this chapter, for more information.

- **Coupons and other promotional items**. You can provide printable coupons and contests or giveaways to customers who "Like" your page. Two things to remember here: First, make sure that you take down expired coupons and contest notices. Second, some people may un-Like your page after they print the coupons or enter the contest. Therefore, make sure that you offer a prize that's relevant for the audience you want to attract and provide content that keeps them engaged even when the contest is over.

In March of 2014, Facebook announced that it was rolling out a newly designed layout for Facebook pages that provides users with more options. The designs vary for online and offline businesses.

3.4 Facebook Groups

Facebook groups are set up by users and are used to discuss topics of interest and express their points of view. In order to join a group, you have to be invited by another member. Facebook groups have begun to wane in popularity with the rise of Facebook Pages. Groups are mostly used because they can offer the privacy that Pages cannot. As a brand, it's better for you to have a page than manage a group, which is really designed for user to user interaction only.

You can market directly in the Facebook groups, but you can certainly identify the ones in which your brand is being discussed extensively. In some cases, you may want to observe the conversation, learn from it, and maybe participate as a social media marketing voice when and where appropriate.

3.5 Facebook Events

If you're holding an event for your customers, employees, or business partners, you can promote it on Facebook by listing it as an event. This can be a virtual or physical event supporting your company, its products, special promotions, or milestones. People can be invited to attend the event as you invite them from within Facebook, either on your mobile or computer. Also the event page can include content about your event, your brand, as well as your products and services.

Conferences, product previews, and special promotions are popularly highlighted through Facebook events. After the event is complete, you can share photos and write-ups of the event on the event page.

If the event is a virtual one in real time, you can do a lot to encourage visitors by creating posts that tease about the event beforehand. You can have different types of events, such as an online Q&A session with a guest, or questions about your latest product. People who use Facebook often appreciate the opportunity to stay there to get answers to their questions from their mobile device or computer. They don't have to make a call or log in to another online chat service. If you wish to stream video events in real time on Facebook, you can also use the Facebook live feature.

3.6 Facebook Applications

Creating pages and events that are supported by advertisements and sponsored stories may not be enough. Some companies choose to build applications that can be installed in a user's profile or on a Facebook page. For a branded application to be a success, it must engage users in a meaningful fashion, whether its purpose is utility or entertainment. The most successful applications can take weeks to build and promote within Facebook, so don't expect this to be a simple endeavor.

Popular applications include games, quizzes, badges, calculators, and tools that analyze a person's social graph, which is a mapping of people and how they relate to each other. For example, TripAdvisor's Cities I've Visited application lets you show your friends which cities around the world you've visited. It has been an extremely popular application. For more information on building Facebook applications, visit the Facebook Developers page (http://developers.facebook.com)

For a list of top Facebook applications you can use a marketer, check out the Ignite Visibility article (https://ignitevisibility.com/10-top-facebook-apps-for-marketers/).

3.7 Facebook Connect/Login with Facebook

Facebook Connect has continued to evolve since its introduction in 2008 and is now commonly referred to as Login with Facebook. In a nutshell, when you use an application that allows you to use Login with Facebook, you have the ability to bring your Facebook social graph to a third-party website. In this case, the social graph is composed of your Facebook network. This means that when users log in to those sites with their Facebook credentials, they can see which of their friends have participated on that website in some fashion, whether by commenting, rating, or writing a product review. Whatever the users do is also sent to Facebook and appears in the Newsfeed of all their friends. But the Newsfeed has some lag time, whereas users can instantly see what their friends are up to by looking at the ticker on the right side of the page.

The ticker allows users to share their activity on third-party websites with their friends in Facebook, which inadvertently gives the site more exposure and greater power from a recommendation perspective. For more information about Login with Facebook, visit the Facebook developers' page (developers.facebook.com).

3.8 The Use of Ads on Facebook

Social media marketing on Facebook is as simple as using Facebook Ads. Facebook has seen the value of advertising on its platform and has worked to enhance this aspect over the years with changes such as Facebook Insights. This built-in statistics tool helps marketers to understand and target their audience based on demographics, user interests, and other essential keywords.

When you start advertising on Facebook, you can immediately see the changes in your reach as you further narrow down and filter your criteria. You also have the option to add ways for your users to interact with the ad, including asking viewers to rate the ad or become a fan of the brand on the platform.

You can also have the viewer of your ad see who amongst their friends are fans of or have endorsed your brand in the past. This strategy is a simple but clever way to catch more consumers' attention.

You can buy Facebook Ads on a cost-per-click (CPC) or a cost-per-impression (CPM) basis. These have been very popular with small businesses because it would allow you to settle on a daily budget and just generally don't cost too much.

You should consider using the following Facebook Ad formats:

1. **Sponsored stories**

Sponsored stories appear with a title, content, and images, and they look and feel like a story. They appear on the right side of the page and may link to a Facebook page or even to your company's website. It is usually recommended that you link to a Facebook page and keep the user within Facebook itself. The sponsored stories are targeted through profile data like the social advertisements and are popular because they're highly visible.

The Newsfeed is what a user first sees when they log into Facebook. The ads appear on the right side (not in the news stream) but are easily noticed.

A variation on the sponsored story is the sponsored video, which functions in a similar fashion. The sponsored videos are popular because they don't require the user to leave the News Feed to view them. You can learn more about these at www.facebook.com/ads/stories.

1. **Advertising your apps**

If you've spent the time and money to create an app, you'll probably want to advertise it. Facebook has two specific types of ads to target to your app. These ads are designed to encourage app engagement and to increase app installations. To begin the process and see how they are created, check out https://developers.facebook.com/products/ads/.

Chapter 4

Twitter

4.0 Introduction

Scarcely any social platform has had progressively intense development over the most recent couple of years than Twitter, the microblogging administration. Twitter (www.twitter.com) is like a blogging administration, then again, actually you're constrained to 280 characters (extended from the first 140) per message, or tweet. Likewise, just individuals who tail you on Twitter see your tweets in their Twitter course of events. You answer to other individuals' tweets, forward their tweets, or send them direct messages. Every one of your supporters sees your tweets.

Today, Twitter has roughly 326 million dynamic clients around the globe, 69 million of whom are in the United States. A larger number of individuals make accounts on Twitter than they do on some other social platform — 135,000 new clients consistently. Dissimilar to on Facebook, the biggest web-based life platform, Twitter clients are commonly more established. Despite the fact that the absolute number of Twitter clients is not exactly Facebook clients, it is developing so quickly and has such a persuasive client base.

You can market on Twitter using paid and unpaid methods. You can buy specific Twitter ad products that allow you to draw attention to your Twitter account, attach yourself to specific trends, and align with certain keyword searches. Third-party services let you also buy attention by associating with celebrities.

But in a similar fashion to Facebook, marketing on Twitter must start with the basic unpaid tactics. And as you do that, remember that Twitter is most powerful for building and nurturing relationships between people, even more so than Facebook. It's because you're limited to 280 characters. When marketing through Twitter, focus tightly on building the relationships, and everything else will follow. Don't worry too much about pushing messages to the community. But when you have to, there are smart ways to do that via the Twitter ad products that don't hurt your reputation in the community.

In this chapter, we'll start with covering the basics of how to get yourself started on Twitter. From there, we'll discuss how you can go about engaging with the Twitter community for unpaid marketing, and then paid marketing tactics. Lastly, we've got some tips and tricks that we'd love to share with you!

4.1 Figuring Out Twitter

In case you're not quite familiar with Twitter, it's essentially a communication platform that was originally inspired by SMS (short message service, or texting) and Facebook. On it, you publish short tidbits of thought or information (called "tweets") within only 280 characters. These tweets can be viewed by other Twitter users and you can view others' tweets as well. In order to have this reciprocal relationship, you simply need to "follow" each other on the platform. Unlike being Facebook friends, when you follow people on Twitter, they're not automatically made to reciprocate in return.

Another difference between Facebook and Twitter is that on the latter, your profile is open to the public by default. This means that anyone can view your tweets, which is really the ideal for a brand or company. On Facebook, your personal profile is usually only viewable by your friends. Because a majority of tweets are public, the more than 500 million tweets sent daily are a treasure trove of information for marketers to learn how consumers communicate and interact online.

Below are some of the basic actions you can take on Twitter:

- **Mentions**: As a user on Twitter, you can publish tweets as soon as you've signed up. Just type in your tweet and you're on your way. To "mention" another user, you can refer to their account in your tweet by preceding their account name with the @ symbol. For example, to mention the Pepsi Twitter account in a tweet, you would need to type @pepsi. Then when a user clicks the Pepsi handle (@pepsi), they will automatically be taken to the Pepsi Twitter page.

• **Retweets**: Another unique feature of Twitter is the ability to retweet someone else's tweet. Think of this as a Forward button. You can retweet by clicking the Retweet button that's below every tweet in your Twitter feed. If someone has tweeted something interesting and you want to share it with your own followers, the Retweet button is the one to use.

Messages: Through Twitter, you can also send direct messages to specific users. These messages are private and seen only by the Twitter user it's addressed to and not by anyone else. To send a direct message to someone who is already following you, begin your tweet by typing D, and follow that with the @ sign and the person's account name. For example, to send a direct message to John, type D @John followed by the actual message. Direct messaging is useful when you want to communicate directly with a customer in response to something they may have tweeted.

• **Hashtags**: Preceded by a hash (#) mark, the hashtag is used for spontaneous categories by people who want to participate in a conversation around a specific topic. For example, during the Super Bowl, people who want to tweet about the game include #superbowl in their tweet. Then, whenever people search for or click on #superbowl, they see all the tweets related to the game. Clicking a hashtag allows a user to see all the other tweets related to that category.

- **Photos and videos**: Recently, Twitter has made it easy to attach a photo that can be seen below your tweet. You just need to click the camera icon when typing your tweet. If you want to display a video, it's the exact same process. Currently, Twitter supports videos that are 2 minutes and 20 seconds long or shorter.

4.2 A Twitter handle

Taking ownership of your brand on Twitter is very important. Sign up on Twitter with your brand or company's name as the Twitter handle so that your customers can easily find and recognize you. If no one has used your company's name, you are lucky. Use this account to communicate company or brand news, special promotions, and product offers; you can also respond to questions, and resolve customer service issues.

If you do not immediately take ownership of your company or brand name on Twitter, someone else may do so on your behalf. This could be a competitor, another business with a similar name, a customer, or a fan. If that happens, you'll probably have to spend a lot of time (and maybe money, too) to get back the username. Most Twitter users automatically associate your brand name on Twitter with your company. Many may not realize that the person behind the Twitter account using your company name is not actually from your company - and that could damage your brand's reputation if that user tweets unprofessional, provoking, or controversial statements.

You'll also want to make sure that you're "verified" on Twitter. To be verified means that *you* are the official representative account for the company. Users will be able to see that you're verified if you have a blue check mark next to your name. To get verified, all you need to do is visit the verification form on Twitter when signing up. In some cases, you may be asked to provide official ID and other information for the platform to be able to check that it's really you.

Now, should you follow every person who follows you? It's good Twitter protocol to do so if you're looking to build relationships with lots of people. If your goal is just customer service, don't feel the need to follow everyone.

However, when you do consider following someone, watch out for spam and viruses. Both spam and viruses have made their way onto the Twitter platform, and probably the easiest way to put your account at risk is to follow another account that is then used to send you links to viruses. So when you choose to follow other people, make sure that they're legitimate people and not spambots or virus malware. It's easy enough to do, too - just click on their profile and look at the kind of content they're tweeting. Red flags to look out for are Twitter handles with long, randomized characters, no profile pictures, and senseless tweets that are just links (and don't click on those links!).

4.3 Preparing for Twitter Marketing

What we've discussed so far covers setting up your account and how you can communicate with the rest of the Twitter community. What comes next is how you can now prepare both yourself *and* your account to engage with current and potential customers.

4.3.1 Twitter searches

For anyone looking to market via Twitter, the first step is to monitor the conversations for your company, brand, and product mentions. You want to know *how* people are talking about you. You can set up these searches easily within Twitter itself or by using a separate application like TweekDeck. Make sure to track not just your company's brand but also your competitors' brands. You'll probably learn more from people talking about your competitors than from their conversations about you. You can use the Twitter search engine or one of the real time engines like Social Mention or Twazzup. You could also try TweetBeep, which gives you Twitter alerts via email on an hourly basis - this'll help you stay on top of everything that happens.

The reason for using a platform like Social Mention or Twazzup is that you can find sorted information in real time. When you use Twitter search, you get a deluge of tweets that you have to sort through. The tweets may be current or a bit older. When you use the real time search engines, you get up-to-the-minute tweets that can be sorted by category. These are the best tools to use for real time marketing campaigns.

4.3.2 Responding to tweets

It's not enough to just listen in on the conversations, though. You have to participate in the conversations, too. This means responding to questions directly addressed to your Twitter username, whether the questions are customer service-related or more general. It also means watching your brand mentions and correcting misinformation (although you don't want to appear defensive when you do this because it can backfire), providing helpful advice when and where appropriate, and broadening relationships with the people who are talking about your company.

Part of being a good social voice is allowing your own personality to shine through, which means opening up and being willing to talk about your own life and not just the brand you represent.

But there can be challenges in being personable and open, too. For example, if you're a mass brand with lots of followers on Twitter and lots of people talking about you, you may have a hard time responding to everyone. It can become cumbersome and resource intensive. Worse still, it may make your Twitter account look like a series of individual responses versus being one that balances responses with fresh, original content.

Managing such a situation can be difficult. If your company receives lots of customer service queries, you may set up a separate Twitter handle to manage those. Similarly, if your brand has lots of consumers asking questions, you may want to create FAQ pages on your website and direct your consumers to those pages. Answering everything completely via Twitter may not always be possible, especially when you're restricted to 280 characters per tweet!

Keep in mind that when your customers talk about your brand, they may not always expect or demand a response from you. Knowing when to join Twitter conversations about your brand and, more importantly, how to do so is very much an art. Don't try to join every conversation, and at the same time, don't ignore all conversations. Try to understand the people behind the conversations, think about whether you can add value to it, and then choose to join or not.

4.3.3 Following and followers

The core of activity on Twitter is following other people and getting followed yourself. First and foremost, make sure that you consider following anyone who follows you. Second, consider following all the employees at your company who have Twitter accounts. You'll build goodwill with them, and they'll generate followers for you.

Next, identify influential tweeters who have large followings, and set about following and establishing relationships with them. These people are similar to influential bloggers. They could be experts in a specific domain, with large audiences who can encourage people to follow you and who can influence others. In some cases, they may not be experts but rather celebrities of one kind or another. Friend or Follow (https://friendorfollow.com/twitter/most-followers/) has a list of the most popular people on Twitter by follower count. Not surprisingly, many of them are celebrities, starting with Katy Perry and Justin Bieber. Next on the list are President Obama, Rihanna, Taylor Swift, Lady Gaga, Ellen DeGeneres, Cristiano Ronaldo, YouTube, and Justin Timberlake.

Different applications can help you identify these users, but one we like that measures a user's influence is called Twitalyzer (www.twitalyzer.com). You may want to also try WeFollow (www.wefollow.com), which is a popular Twitter directory that helps you find interesting and influential people and brands to follow. When deciding who to follow, think about it like a cocktail party. First, start with the people you know and the people that they know, and then people talking about subjects important to you, and finally random (or influential!) people and those who approach you.

4.3.4 Marketing via Twitter

At this point, you've done the research on how the Twitter community is talking about you, you've gained a significant following, and you've done *just* the right amount of engagement with your followers. The world of Twitter knows who you are (or at least has an inkling), what you do, and why they need to follow you. That means you can start marketing your products in a more targeted way, starting with how you can do that for free before moving on to the paid tactics.

You can use Twitter to market in a number of ways, but there are a few more urgent and critical ways that you should do so. We list those ways here in order of what we think you should prioritize:

1. **Listening to customers**: Twitter is an incredible platform for you to figure out how your clients consider your items, your organization, and the general business that you're in. Try not to pass up on the chance to tune in to your clients talk about your image progressively. Listen genuinely to your client's worries and utilize the platform to react specifically.
2. **Promoting product launches and events**: Getting news around fast is essential in marketing your products, and there's no social media platform that spreads news faster than Twitter does. Because of this, marketers have the ability to use Twitter in an efficient way to share products and market events to profit on the purpose of the sharing of ads. In fact, marketing efforts can be shared in this manner. For example, certain big-name brands who have celebrity endorsements in new ads can have these celebrities announce its release on their respective Twitter accounts. A recent example would be the Pepsi

commercials for the 2019 Super Bowl. One features singer Cardi B, and she didn't waste any time promoting it on her own Twitter.

3. **Making special deals and discounts**: Promos and discounts are often collaborated with the use of Twitter. Clients answers fast to these Twitter offers and usually disseminate the word to their own followers - retweeting makes that so much easier. Some companies have set up special deal accounts through which they tweet about deals. One example of a company setting up a special deals handle for tweeting about deals on a regular basis is @delloutlet. The Dell Outlet twitter handle has approximately 1.17 million Twitter followers.

4. **Customer service**: Companies use Twitter as an alternative customer service option. They listen for customer complaints and respond to those customers via Twitter itself, or at the very least, they begin the response on Twitter before moving to a phone call or an email exchange. Comcast, JetBlue, and Home Depot are all examples of companies that have successfully used Twitter for customer service.

5. **Engaging meaningfully with customers**: Different companies take different approaches to engaging in a meaningful way with their customers via Twitter. Nike has a separate account, @NikeSupport, that encourages its community to support each other as well as provide customer support. Whole Foods provides healthful recipes. It also asks its customers what they like to read and watch and then recommends new food podcasts and invites the customers to upcoming company or in-store events.

4.3.5 Promoted accounts on Twitter

Twitter has a huge number of items for publicizing that empower and enable advertisers to achieve clients all the more viably by means of their platform. Among the first of these accessible to publicists are Promoted Accounts, which attracts consideration regarding your Twitter account. In the event that you become tied up with a Promoted Account, you will find in the Who to Follow region your Twitter account name shows up at the correct side of the Twitter screen, with "Advanced" subtitled beneath it.

These Promoted Accounts urge other Twitter clients to pursue your record. You can target who you need to see your Promoted Account by means of a couple of things, for example, topography, interests, and profile portrayals. Advanced Accounts are estimated one of two different ways, which you get the opportunity to choose. They are valued either on an impression premise, which implies that you'll pay for the quantity of individuals who see the Promoted Account posting, or by the quantity of individuals who tail you. The last clearly can differ colossally relying upon purchaser intrigue levels.

While having the most noteworthy number of devotees on Twitter is anything but a genuine proportion of accomplishment, it is significant to develop a solid base of supporters. This will enable you to proceed to fabricate and change over others as they associate with you on the platform.

Promoted Accounts have the additional benefit that after people become your followers, they typically stay your followers. This lasting value differs from display advertising, for which a dollar spent on an impression is lost after the ad campaign has run. You get no real long term benefit from that investment.

4.3.6 Making use of promoted tweets

Promoted Tweets let you draw even more attention to just a single tweet. These Promoted Tweets are mainly sold by being associated to a particular search term. You can select to add a layer focusing on advancement all together for the tweets to contact the general population you truly need to reach.

SOCIAL MEDIA MARKETING AND PERSONAL BRANDING

Beneath you will see the distinctive kinds of Promoted Tweets, and what they are best for:

• **Promoted Tweets in a search**: This is best used to target clients who don't yet tail you or a brand on Twitter. When utilizing this item, you can achieve individual clients through a predetermined pursuit term along these lines to the manner in which Google enables you to promote per the inquiries on its site Google look. Remember that a particular sponsor can buy an inquiry term at any irregular time. Advanced Tweets are purchased through a sale display. Regularly amid the long stretches of an evening, you could see multiple brands competing with one another in real time by buying Promoted Tweets and using the identical search term. In this way, they try to outbid each other for the customer's attention. Promoted Tweets are popular because they allow brands to attach themselves most directly to consumer intent. For example, if you search tweets about holidays, airlines know that you'll probably be thinking about flights, too, and that it is valuable for them to advertise using that phrase.

• **Targeting followers**: Promoted tweets can be used to target followers of your brand on Twitter as well. You may wonder why you should use ads to target followers when they're already following you. But the reality is that when you tweet to your followers, your tweet quickly drops below the fold and can be missed by your followers. When you use Promoted Tweets to target followers, the promoted tweet stays at the top of the feed. As a result, it becomes practically impossible for the follower to miss the tweet.

Promoted tweets are valuable when you want to promote something to your followers — the people who are typically your biggest brand advocates. This strategy works well when you have something to share that you believe will spread organically after it's seeded to a small group of brand loyalists.

• **Geotargeting**: Promoted tweets get even more powerful when you geo-target them at the country or even the DMA level (Nielsen-designated market areas). When you target a Promoted Tweet to just the people in specific locations that matter to you, your Promoted Tweet costs get much lower. This matters most for local businesses who care to advertise only in the actual locations where their businesses exist. Geotargeting can be applied as a layer over any kind of Promoted Tweets.

Promoted Tweets are bought on a cost-per-engagement (CPE) basis versus a cost-per-thousand-impressions (CPM) basis. CPE means that you pay only when a user retweets, replies, clicks, or favorites your tweet. You won't pay for the number of users or people who see the tweet but for those who do something about it or click something because of it. Paying for everyone who saw your tweet alone would be paying on a CPM basis. This fee style creates a system where promoted tweets are very cost effective, and are a performance-based form of spending on social media marketing. It is also for many marketers a nice complement to the many different forms of digital marketing.

4.3.7 Using promoted trends

Twitter is a hopeful internet-based platform for different reasons. However, one component that is significant on Twitter is the manner by which "drifting" subjects work. Each minute inconsistently, Twitter dissects the majority of many discussions occurring on its platform and figures out what is prominent or drifting in a specific minute.

The inclining points you will see get highlighted by the client's feed on the left side. They can be separated by topography too, so for instance, you can see just the drifting points in your general vicinity like the United States or notwithstanding inclining subjects that are imperative just to specific urban communities. What is drifting on Twitter goes about as a gauge of how much a thing might be topical in the physical world at some random minute. Drifting themes are unquestionably not to be missed.

Advanced Trends supplement the natural patterns and help brands to assemble mass mindfulness, influence declarations, to promote item dispatches, talk about occasions coming up, and develop their image by the relationship with other social occasions. They work along these lines to drifting points with the exception of Promoted Trends that are characterized by the publicists. A client sees the Promoted Trend on the left half of the screen with the other slanting themes yet with the word Promoted beneath it.

As with Promoted Tweets, clients can click Promoted Trends to see every one of the tweets containing a certain hashtag or pattern terms related with that Promoted Trend. Tapping the Promoted puts a user to a search results page that possesses a Paid Tweet from the advertiser at the top of it. Other tweets on the search results page will be unfiltered and open.

Promoted Trends are typically most valuable to buy on days when major pop culture events are happening and then best when aligned in some meaningful form around those pop culture events. For example, when the VMAs (Video Music Awards) air on TV, you might want to buy a Promoted Trend about music or, more specifically, about an award-winning artist from the VMAs because a lot of people will be on Twitter talking about the VMAs.

Promoted Trends are extremely popular with marketers, and it is worth buying the Promoted Trend in advance of the actual day that you want it to run. This is essential because only one Promoted Trend can run on Twitter on a given day, marketers buy those terms well in advance of the actual day that they want the ad to run.

4.3.8 Working with sponsored tweets

One other current advertising opportunity that blends into the paid-tactics domain is Sponsored Tweets. In a similar fashion to sponsored posts on Wogs, some Twitter users with very large followings are open to publishing Sponsored Tweets. Sponsored Tweets are done by speaking directly to Twitter users and securing their interest in posting. You discuss the marketing campaign with willing users and they tweet about your campaign in their own language and style to their own audiences.

Typically, Twitter users publish Sponsored Tweets only if they can disclose the fact that they're sponsored, and if the marketing messages are in sync with their own personal brand and the type of information that they like to share with their followers. Sponsored tweeting is an emergent marketing tactic. An example of a company that provides this service is Sponsored Tweets at http://sponsoredtweets.com/.

4.4 Tips and tricks

Twitter is an adaptable platform and advertisers use it in a wide range of approaches to accomplish their showcasing and business targets. Truth be told, the adaptability of Twitter is the thing that has made it such a significant platform for advertisers. Some utilize it principally for to explore clients, some to advance explicit advertising programs, some for an effort to become influencers, and others for client administration.

Despite how you use it, Twitter causes you to assemble a steadfast, submitted base of adherents. You should remember some key tips and traps when utilizing Twitter to drive up your computerized commitment with them:

- *Provide worth to your customers.*

It is anything but difficult to overlook that Twitter wasn't created as a commitment platform for advertisers to use as an interface with their clients. Or maybe, it was created for individuals to interface with one another, realize what their companions are doing, and communicate their own exercises. For brands to take an interest seriously, they should increase the value of the experience; else, they will be overlooked.

- *Keep in mind that different strategies make sense for different marketing needs.*

Remember that your Twitter procedure needs to line up with your general advertising system. On an instance that your business is about client administration, use Twitter for client administration. If it is for providing exclusive access, use Twitter as a distribution engine for promoting how you provide exclusive access. Match the Twitter tactics to the marketing strategy.

- *Prepare to adjust your Twitter approach.*

There's no better way to evolve your Twitter approach than by paying attention to how your customers respond to your participation during social conversations. Learn from them, and adjust your Twitter approach based on what you see working effectively in real time. Are your customers responding to questions posed by you? Do they shy away from talking about your product? Are they more interested in learning about future marketing activities? Use their participation as a guide for how to market on Twitter.

- *Use Twitter advertising to jump-start conversations.*

Nothing beats organic engagement on Twitter. To be able to hear from your customers in real time, participate in conversations with them, and watch them go about their lives through the conversations that they have on the platform is extremely powerful. However, there are times when you need to use the mass reach of paid advertising to jump-start those engagements or draw special attention to what you're doing. Twitter advertising products help that process.

- *Remember that knowing your customers is as important as ever.*

Some marketers make the mistake of believing that simply because this is a 280-character communication format, you don't need to know your customers as well. That's not true. Before you respond to a tweet from a customer, take a minute to understand who that customer is, what else they tweet about, and what matters to them.

- *Listen, listen, and listen.*

It may be a cliché, but it's still very true. Listening to how your customers talk to each other about culture, about your products' category, your products, and your company is critical to succeeding on Twitter. Listening is the first step in participating in conversations — a step that must not be skipped.

On a final note, you can also make use of what is called Twitter Cards. The cards provide a summary of your Twitter business information along with your tweet. They require a bit of html to be added to your website.

Hopefully, you now understand how Twitter could be potentially beneficial in the promotion of your brand and your products.

Chapter 5

Instagram

5.0 Introduction

Whether you are a newbie to Instagram or not, you still stand to learn a lot from this chapter, especially when it comes to applying it to marketing. If you *are* new to the application, though, learning about it here will probably convince you to finally give it a try. It has, after all, made big waves since its release in 2010 and it's a feat that you've been able to stay off it for this long!

In July 2012, Instagram's growth blew up even more when it was acquired by Facebook. Similar to Pinterest and Tumblr, Instagram is a platform that allows its users to share visual content with incredible ease. It also kind of serves as a photo editor since you have a range of photo filters to choose from when editing before posting. The main difference between Instagram and Tumblr or Pinterest is that Instagram focuses on users' and marketers' original content whereas the other two are primarily images that are already online and shared amongst the community.

In this chapter, we'll go over the basics of Instagram before moving on to how both personal users and marketers can use it to build a relationship with the community. You'll learn more about editing photos, developing a storyline, discovering others, and getting yourself discovered.

5.1 Instagram for The Uninitiated

Instagram is primarily a mobile application, though it is also viewable on computers. However, it's better utilized on mobile, as it's much easier to snap photos and post them immediately from there. The first step, then, is to download the application for your iOS, Android, or Windows gadgets.

That is, you should download the application when you're sure that you can reach your target demographic using this platform. To help you determine that a little easier, let's take a look at the 2019 statistics projection reported by Hootsuite:

Instagram has 1 billion users, 50% of whom use the platform every day.

80% of users are located outside the U.S.

60% of users have discovered products on Instagram.

72% of users have bought a product they've seen on Instagram.

In its report called "Social Media 2013 Update," Pew Research says that:

Twenty percent of female U.S. adults and 15 percent of male adults use Instagram.

The largest user age group is 18-29.

If this sounds like the audience that you want to reach, you need to jump on the platform right away! Join the 25% of the Fortune 500 companies that also consider Instagram vital in their own marketing campaigns.

According to a study by L2-Intelligence, about 93% of luxury brands like Cartier, Chanel, Dior, Calvin Klein, and Versace are on Instagram. If you take a quick look at their profiles, you'll see that they are able to produce high quality visual content that looks great on their profile page. As a company, that's exactly what you're aiming for too!

5.1.1 Signing up

So after you've downloaded the application onto your device, you need to set up your account. Register with your email or Facebook account, though we personally suggest the former so it's more professional. It's as easy as that! You can choose to make your account public or private, but for purpose of this chapter, we're using the model of a public Instagram account (since you don't want a company account that's private).

5.1.2 Exploring the app

Take a look at the bottom of your screen when you open up the application. You'll see a few icons that'll take you to different places in the app. Here's a brief rundown of what these icons mean:

- **Home**: This is where you see all photos posted by the people you follow.

- **Explore**: Here you can search for topics of interest or see what the app recommends for you based on who you follow.

- **Camera**: What you click when you want to take a photo directly from the app. You can either take a new one, or choose from those already in your device's photo library.

- **Following**: This is where you see your followers' activity - who recently followed you, liked or commented on your posts, or new posts in hashtags you recently viewed.

- **Your photos**: Photos you have taken and uploaded to instagram.

5.1.3 Using filters

As we mentioned earlier, Instagram has its own filters that you can use to edit your photos. Of course, you can also leave your photos as it is, that's entirely up to you. In fact, it was reported that 50% of users do not use any of the filters.

The filters give the photos a specific effect, like making it brighter or darker, enhancing the warm and cool undertones, or rendering it completely black and white. The top five filters used on Instagram as of this writing are Normal, EarlyBird, X-Pro II, Valencia, and Rise. You may also opt to use other photo-taking or editing apps to get the effect you desire before posting them onto Instagram.

Other advanced in-app parameters which will help you enhance or upgrade your filters are as follows:

- **Filters**: The filters now have a slider that allows you to see how much of the effect you want to apply.

- **Vignette**: In addition to the Tilt-Shift tool, you can now use the Vignette tool to create a blurry black border around the photo.

- **Cropping and straightening**: You can use these photos to cut your photos to your desired size, or maybe even tilt it a little off-center.

5.1.4 Getting Found on Instagram

You're all set up now and can navigate your way around the app. So what's next, you ask? What's next is that you want to be discovered.

Who doesn't love a good hashtag? What started on Twitter has migrated to Instagram, and it really helps you get found. On Instagram though, some people can really get carried away with their hashtags. Every social media platform has its own unspoken guidelines for hashtags - obviously on Twitter it's limited because of the character count, and Facebook doesn't really *have* a hashtag culture. However, Instagram embraces hashtags, so you can use them to your heart's content. Just remember that as a business, you should choose your hashtags wisely.

Hashtags are vital in a marketing campaign as they will help you really expand your reach, even to those who aren't already in your community of followers. It will also make it easier for you to track how people are engaging with your brand, especially if you have hashtags customized for your company.

For these reasons, it is prudent for you to look at what hashtags are currently being used and what new ones you should create. One way to find out this information is to look at search tools for hashtags. Some of these hashtag tools include:

1. **Talkwalker** (http://talkwalker.com): Free/Fee versions. This tool has lots of value. You can see the performance of a hashtag and much more; for example, you can see the influencers who use it and whether the sentiment about it is positive or negative.
2. **RiteTag** (http://ritetag.com): Free! One of the great features of this tool is that it will go over the hashtags you have used in Twitter and tell you whether they are overused or unlikely to be seen. Obviously, you won't use this tool for a new Instagram campaign.
3. **Tagboard** (https://tagboard.com): Free/Fee versions. What's so useful about this tool is that you can build tagboards that display specific hashtags, making it easy to see what's happening.

Check these out to see how helpful it can be to analyze and evaluate your hashtags.

5.1.5 Structuring Instagram for Business Goals

As you can see, Instagram is a social media giant that has enormous potential for almost every business. An obvious clue to its value is that it was purchased by and is highly integrated with Facebook. Many small and medium-sized marketers have yet to take advantage of it, though. One reason is that they are already overwhelmed by the number of social media platforms that they feel required to use.

Don't be one of these marketers. Look carefully at which platforms you choose to devote your time and budget to. If a platform is large but not right for your user base, don't get pulled into using it because everyone uses it. If you feel that you can build relevant and engaging visual content for your brand, then Instagram is a great place to set up a social media marketing campaign.

5.1.6 Creating Content For Your Business

As with any social platform you choose, you want to develop relationships with a community of like-minded people who can become your customers. On Instagram, images serve as the main tool and the stories they tell.

To help your team focus on uploading the right images for the company, it's helpful to create a list of category stories to which your staff can refer. You want your staff to easily generate new photos and videos and not miss the great moments to capture.

For example, some story categories could be the following:

- **Working in the community**: pictures of charity events and training sessions with users.

- **Community member photos**: encourage users to send in photos depicting their use of the product.

- **Our pets at work**: Adorable pet photos that humanize your staff and make connections with other pet lovers who can upload their photos.

- **Contests**: Photos of contest entries by users and winner photos.

- **Featured staff members**: Video of staff members giving a video greeting (fifteen seconds long at most).

- **Request for product improvements**: Photos of current products with questions from the company about how to improve them. Customers are asked to reply to these questions and offer some ideas of their own.

- **Inspiring photos just because**: A beautiful image from nature or daily life to make others feel good.

Engaging users by using consistent story themes is the best approach. When users see a new image, they can relate it to all the other images that have made up that storyline for your brand. This creates a "series" feeling that keeps visitors coming back for more. Think of it like a TV show with particular stories that are continually updated.

Here are two other items that your staff should pay attention to:

1. **Hashtags**: As discussed earlier, hashtags are how people find your content. Make sure to use ones that are already in use that relate to your brand. Using them is a habit people already have. In addition, create specific hashtags for your brand.
2. **Captions**: Every photo should have a caption. We are trained to look for them and read them. Therefore, captions are an important part of the marketing process on Instagram. Don't assume that they are optional. Users have been shown to favor long ones, so give careful thought to what you write. Be creative!

5.1.7 Curating and Sharing

Key to everything you do on Instagram is the idea that sharing will create buzz and new followers. Hand-in-hand with content creation is the manner in which you share it to your audience. As we said, you are presenting stories. The best way to do that pretty much speaks for itself on Instagram - by using the platform's Stories feature.

5.2 Instagram stories

In August 2016, Instagram launched what is probably their most successful feature to date - Instagram Stories. In today's fast-paced world, not everyone has time to spend hours and hours browsing through apps like Instagram - no matter how beautiful all the photos are. With the Stories feature, brands now have around 10 to 15 seconds to basically pitch whatever they're advertising - themselves, their products, or what-have-you. Your Stories are posted immediately to the Homepage of everyone who follows you.

As a marketer, there are many ways that you can take advantage of this. Because you can post photos *and* videos, there's really no limit to the content that you can create. You can post a plain background with bold text that advertises your next contest or a clickable link to your website; you can post short videos showing a glimpse of how your products are made - the possibilities are endless!

In 2018, Instagram added even more features to Stories that allow you to make more dynamic, interactive posts. Some of these include:

- **Clickable links**: Viewers can be redirected immediately to your blog, website, or even another account when they click on the links.

- **Polls**: You can put an interactive poll on your Stories to immediately engage your customers and gain insight. For example, you could ask about opinions on color combinations on products, or what dish they'd like to see cooked up next. Your poll could be about anything curated to your brand.

- **Quick reactions**: Viewers can now react to your video immediately, without having to leave a comment or direct message. This is useful to marketers in order to discover whether users love or hate that specific advertisement.

- **Auto video segmentation**: When the feature first launched, users needed to rush to fit everything into the 15-second limit. Now, you can post longer videos and the app will automatically split it up into 15-second increments for you - it's seamless and effortless, and you don't need to rush through any dialogue or text to force it to fit.

- **Share to Stories**: This is very useful in customer engagement. You're now able to share other people's content to your Stories, where it will link back to the original content. So, if you're doing cross-promotional content with other users or brands, this is great! Or if a customer posts an A++ amazing review about your brand, you can share it to your Stories so that your other followers can see how amazing you are. Think of it as similar to retweeting.

One potentially problematic aspect of Instagram Stories when it was introduced was that it would only appear on your followers' Homepage for 24 hours before it's archived. However, this problem was solved in December 2017 with Instagram Highlights.

5.2.1 Instagram highlights

In order for Instagram stories not to disappear after a day, Instagram introduced the Highlights feature. Users are now able to save their stories to specifically curated galleries on their profiles.

So taking from the examples in the previous section for story categories, a company could have one Highlight focused on "Community Work", another for "Featured Employee", and yet another for "Contests". There's no limit to the number of Highlights you can create, but you can only have 100 Stories per Highlight.

By making use of the Highlights feature, your followers can keep coming back to your Stories if they need information after 24 hours of it being posted.

5.2.2 IGTV

Instagram TV was also introduced in mid-2018, but it has yet to really take off. IGTV is the YouTube of Instagram and allows you to post long-form content that is specifically produced for the platform. It's not like Facebook Live or Instagram Stories which allows you to stream in real time.

So if you feel that 15 seconds of segmented content on Instagram Stories just doesn't cut it, you might want to consider building a profile on IGTV. Though it is built directly into the Instagram app for viewers, you'll have to download the IGTV app to create and upload content.

If you are creating and displaying only your own pictures and not finding and sharing other people's content, you are talking to, essentially, yourself. You also need to spread other people's stories to demonstrate that you are interested in more than just your own company's activities. If your brand has a strong visual campaign, Instagram is the perfect place for your marketing strategies.

Some brands known for their success on Instagram include Oreo, Nike, Gucci, and WeWork. Check out their profiles if you want an idea for how to build your own Instagram presence!

Chapter 6

YouTube

6.0 Introduction

YouTube is another social platform that has had explosive growth since its launch in 2005. It is now the number one website for online videos and whenever marketers think of viral marketing, they often think in terms of YouTube. You can't afford to overlook it as a marketing vehicle, due to its importance to consumers and its potential reach.

In this chapter, we will discuss briefly about YouTube basics before moving to how you as a marketer can create customized content for your subscribers. We give some tips on how you can interact with your viewers and finally, how you can seed a viral campaign.

6.1 YouTube In One Glance

If you think that YouTube is not a large force in the marketing space, consider the following facts:

If YouTube were a cable network, it would be the largest one.

Approximately 80 percent of the traffic on YouTube is from outside the United States.

YouTube accounts for 28 percent of all Google searches and is the world's second largest search engine after Google.

Mobile views already represent 25 percent of all YouTube video views globally.

Clearly, YouTube has all the muscle you need to drive your *video* social media marketing efforts. You can't afford not to utilize it.

6.2 Why Social Media Marketing on YouTube?

The principal thing you have to ask yourself is the amount of cash you prefer to spend on placing ads on YouTube. You realize that you need to take part, yet you aren't sure how much time or exertion to dedicate to it. To enable you to choose, here are a few advantages you can get from showcasing on YouTube:

- **Visibility**: Most importantly, being on YouTube puts you directly amidst where the activity is. Individuals come to YouTube to search for recordings, and you need your video pieces to be found.

- **Branding**: Stretching out your marking to the recordings you make is really direct. Your logo and other structure things ought to dependably be available, which causes you with brand acknowledgment. On the off chance that you don't have these components, you will need to get them for every social medium advertising endeavors.

- **Fees are not required when setting up**: As opposed to setting up a site, transferring a video on YouTube and making a channel is free. On an instance that you as of now have recordings you've made, everything to do is join. See the area later where we talk about how to "Alter Your YouTube Content". You must also be aware of your expenses like the maintenance of your videos.

- **Fixed placement selections**: You should not be stressed over how your video will look or be set and output on the site. Yours will be shown close by the various recordings. Your objective at that point ought to clearly be the means by which to emerge, not how to fit in. In the event that you have a designer who can utilize the YouTube API to enable you to emerge, then you are in a colossal favorable position.

- **Optimized already for search engines**: Because of the inherent website improvement organization of the webpage,

Google shows your recordings in its query items. In any case, you should give careful consideration to the catchphrases that are utilized to portray recordings with the goal that they get the extra consideration they merit.

6.3 Getting People to Subscribe to Your Channel

Individuals on YouTube who patronize your channel are known as your endorsers. Each time you transfer another video, they get advised, and their names and symbols have appeared to you on your YouTube channel page.

Think about the supporters as your devotees on Twitter and adherents on Instagram or even fans on Facebook pages. Similarly, as you would support those connections on those other social platforms, you ought to do likewise here as well. You will ask, what's the most ideal approach to assemble a bunch of subscribers on Youtube? Consider doing the following:

1. **Quality is better than quantity**.

You've presumably heard that when you are on the web, "quality written substance makes all the difference." Think about your substance for your YouTube channel as you would for a TV channel. On the off chance that the substance is feeble, you won't manufacture a network of endorsers who clatter for additional. It is not required though to have a Hollywood level quality, however you do need to extend a particular polished methodology and consistency.

1. **Great strategies provide better results**

Don't simply consider you are direct as far as one video at any given moment yet rather as a channel where you'll distribute explicit bits of substance all through occasions of the year — some will be instructive, some more for diversion, and some news-centered recordings that offer some incentive to your watchers and construct your image in the meantime.

1. **Promote video commenting**

Remarks on YouTube are much the same as the remarks you'd see on online journals or other internet based life like Facebook. Some have esteem; some are simply senseless or jabber. You will likely make a network of individuals who acknowledge and anticipate your transferred recordings. In case they post remarks that demonstrate that you are satisfying them, you've met your objective.

1. **Subscribe to other people's videos**

There are two qualities in buying in to other individuals' recordings. The first is you get the opportunity to perceive what the experience resembles. You need to see how it feels to buy in and what different ways channel proprietors draw in with their endorsers so you can impersonate this for your very own supporters. Furthermore, it allows you to meet and impart to others on their page. They are keen on getting supporters just as you are as well. Keep in mind, this page is a social platform.

1. **Utilize your videos by sharing it on other platforms**

The main reason why you need to do this is that you will build and get more supporters. It likewise enhances your picture on those different platforms. In any case, as you begin to share your clasps somewhere else, dependably put the video on YouTube first and insert from YouTube as opposed to transferring straightforwardly to the site you're sharing on. The only exemption might be Facebook, where you can transfer specifically and perhaps you'll have higher commission rates with your video by transferring the video straightforwardly to Facebook.

6.4 Promoting on YouTube

Realizing how to distribute and advance your video reach is vital to getting them the consideration they merit. Coming up next are a few suggestions you can follow while advancing your video cuts on YouTube.

Having a committed YouTube channel for your organization or brand is imperative since it enables you to feature all related video cuts in a single spot. A YouTube channel will go about as your image's record home, and where cuts that you have distributed can show up. Setting up a channel is exceptionally simple, so don't hesitate to do such.

A channel likewise gives you a chance to make a profile for yourself and have a spot to interface your site. Make a point to alter the channel to coordinate your organization or your image's visual character. You don't have to physically make your YouTube channel. When you agree to accept a record, utilize the "Make Account" connect in the upper right corner of the landing page, and transfer a video cut. A channel will be naturally made for you. To achieve your YouTube channel, simply click your username after you sign in. It's as simple as that!

In addition, remember to give a connection to and from your site to your YouTube channel. Additionally, ensure that your different channels, similar to your Facebook page and online journals, likewise have connections to your YouTube channel. Complementary connections are critical to a reasonable and brief internet based life showcasing effort.

6.5 Modify your YouTube content

Putting up TV ads on the platform is not enough itself because it will be subpar if you do not modify it according to the style of the format of the platform for it to become effective. It is crucial to optimize the ads to the preference of the viewers at all times.

You must also attempt to limit the time of your videos, preferably fewer than 5 minutes, so that the size of the file will not be too high. In fact, the usual length of a footage is about a little more than 4 minutes. You must also categorize your videos into themed playlist so that it will be much easier to access by people.

For various instances, a quick footage that lasts just a few minutes can have a huge effect. You are trying to get your audience to disseminate your video in the various platforms. This being said, you can't anticipate the viewers to exert a lot of effort on a single video. The fact that the site has a massive number of users and content is enough to explain why it will be a challenge for your content to be seen.

Developers at YouTube seem to have a learned a thing or two from the success of Instagram stories, because they've introduced the exact same feature on YouTube. Creators can now post short Stories that are displayed to their subscribers. As a marketer, you can use these Stories to tease content that's lined up for future release.

6.6 Tag and categorize everything you upload

Like the other social media platforms discussed, YouTube has also introduced the concept of tagging and categorizing its content. Make sure that you choose the best and most appropriate tags and categories for your content! The last thing you want is to be reaching out to the wrong consumers who have no interest or need for your products. Start by looking for videos in your industry and see what tags they're using.

Of course, your content may not be an exact fit in one category but you can resolve this by seeing which category has the most videos similar to yours. Then you can use customized tags to fill up the holes left by the limits in categorization. YouTube lets you add an unlimited number of tags, so your options are literally limitless. These tags, like hashtags, make it easier for users to find your content if they're viewing something similar.

Use YouTube's email and bulletins, too, if that fits in with your company's marketing goals. This will help with the promotion of your clips as email subscribers will receive regular updates about your content or will even recommend you to those viewing similar content as yours. The bulletins and stories feature also allows you to update your current subscribers.

Just be careful that you're not being too spammy, as this'll turn off a lot of subscribers and users. If they haven't asked for an email, don't email them.

6.7 Make response videos

A common way that YouTube content creators interact and expand their reach is by collaborating with each other. One way to do this is to make response videos! You can make use of this strategy with other videos that are in your niche. However, remember to keep it civil and respectful - you're NOT going to do yourself any good if you are judgmental.

Procter and Gamble utilized this system to make impact on its prevalent Old Spice fellow campaign with Isaiah Mustafa. In the first place, the organization made an entertaining video advancing the item. At that point, it followed up by making video reactions by Mustafa to the remarks made on the web. This rose on the ubiquity of the first video and made the watchers return for an additional one. The incredible news about this system is that despite the fact that it's modest, it can pack a punch. Envision the shock of your watchers when you react to their remarks with a video customized for them.

6.8 Include a call to action

Every good commercial on TV should leave you with the feeling that you should go out and buy or do what they told you to do. That particular tactic is called a "call to action". Your YouTube content should be no different - just lose the hard sell and don't be so glaringly obvious about it. Always link back to your site, or slip in a short skit about buying merchandise. You could even include contact details for your viewers to reach out to if they want to learn more or engage in more conversation. This is an opportunity to generate sale, so don't forget your calls to action!

Additionally, unlike TV commercials, there's no need to wait until the end before you include the call to action in your YouTube video. The link can be suspended on a part of the video throughout the whole thing, or you can slip it in halfway - it's all up to you!

6.9 Important Note: Have fun, too!

YouTube is entertainment central - its users flock to the platform seeking videos to entertain them. That means that you, as a creator, should be giving them something entertaining too! Even if the nature of your content is educational or informational, there's never anything wrong with injecting a little bit of humor every now and then. Take a look at the channel Crash Course, which covers all things educational, or BuzzFeed Unsolved's "Ruining History" videos - they're very informational, but it's definitely not a classroom lecture!

When producing your videos, ask yourself if it's something that you would watch - that's always the best way to go. Also remember that the first few seconds are the most crucial in capturing and keeping your audience's attention. Start off energized and try to sustain that, otherwise you'll lose your viewers as your video goes on.

6.10 Creating a Viral Campaign

Viral recordings are of two kinds, and it is vital to be comfortable with them:

1. Organic: This is the kind of video that makes a universal furor, and heaps of individuals hurry to see it and offer it with their companions (for instance: Psy's Korean melody Gangnam Style, which is perhaps the most seen video ever all around, with in excess of 2 billion perspectives). Ordinarily, it simply happens naturally absent much by way of arranging. It catches the creative ability of watchers and goes and detonates.

2. Seeded: This kind of video has a cautiously arranged crusade for turning into a web sensation with especially thought behind it and

publicizing dollars to spend. It may circulate around the web, however, there is no surety. A few organizations have practical experience in influencing recordings to have viral seeding, or you can even go to general web-based social networking offices to get help. Organizations like Sharethrough (www.sharethrough.com), TubeMogul (www.tubemogul.com), and Tubular (www.tubularlabs.com) can help in such manner.

Would you be able to influence a video to turn into a web sensation? Determinedly not. If you can, advertisers would dispatch them by the armload. In any case, these few hints and traps may enhance your odds of making a viral video.

1. Keep the substance new: Nothing beats new substance with regards to making viral video cuts. The substance should be so captivating and extraordinary that individuals can't resist the urge to need to impart it to everybody they know. Continuously begin by concentrating on the substance.

2. Use big names if conceivable: In case you are speaking to a major brand and can utilize big names, use them. Don't speculate about doing that, do it. Adding superstars to the storyline commonly makes the recordings turn out to be progressively popular. We're a big name fixated advanced culture, and VIPs drive sees particularly in popular culture today. It is as fundamental as that. The absolute most mainstream publicizing recordings amid the World Cup, Super Bowl, and other huge brandishing occasions every single utilized VIP.

3. Make it strange: A video that you need to watch a few times over and offer to your companions is typically a video that has a dreamlike component in it. Somebody is accomplishing something in the video that is exceptionally strange or extremely insane and you can't help watch it rehashed occasions or converse with others about it. Better also is if a big name or acclaimed individual is accomplishing something dreamlike.

4. Implore feelings: Brain science has demonstrated that the recordings that draw in the most consideration and are shared most frequently are the ones that entreat feelings in the watcher. This happens regardless of whether those feelings are of wonder, of indignation, about diversion, or about sicken. Albeit some of the time dreamlike recordings are regularly the ones that get shared frequently, don't overlook alternate ways which you could stimulate the feelings of any potential watcher. Also, remember that recordings that beg a scope of feelings are normally the ones that play out the most ideal way since they are progressively multidimensional.

5. Make it short: Individuals online normally don't have much time. You should keep the viral little clasp short. Some of the time cuts as short as ten seconds are sufficiently long for a video to possibly turn into a web sensation. Likewise make sure to concentrate on quality rather than quantity. In addition, recall that there aren't any rigid tenets for what the recommended length of a YouTube video ought to be.

6. Don't make it an advertisement: Commonly, advertisers cannot avoid the impulse to transform pretty much anything into commercial. The substance should be seen and experienced as stimulation. The ideal method to engage an objective client is to consider taking a gander at everything else they are likely review on YouTube and after that utilization those as a benchmark to appreciate what style of substance they would be most inspired by.

You would likewise complete a viral seeding effort on a financial plan. Someone inside your association could be responsible for making a crusade that would be produced. You should pick how high the stakes are and what the general objective is.

Viral seeding is the ability to disseminate footages in a specific niche to improve its share-ability. That can mean including the following:

- **Targeting influencers**: If you have a lot of connections on a certain niche, then you can advertise the content of the videos.

- **Advertising**: Video proprietors purchase various kinds of advertising — Google, YouTube, Facebook, etc. — to elevate the chances of sharing.

- **Creating resonance**: Integrating the videos in a more profound and truthful that everyone can incorporate themselves to will increase the probability of your videos trending.

- **Placing it on social networks**: Connects the footage to Facebook posts, tweets etc.

- **Partnerships**: Partnering with popular YouTubers to aide in promoting the videos can create a lot of improvement.

- **Emailing it to popular lists**: Famous newsletters have the privilege to put a link to the footage.

- **Blogging**: Popular bloggers integrate a link to the footage in some of their posts.

- **Putting up giveaways**: Giving freebies can increase the number of viewers for the footage.

An instance of viral seeding happening is a campaign Unilever made for one of its brands in 2013; Dove. It was in April of that year, Unilever propelled a YouTube video wherein a few ladies portray themselves to a measurable sketch craftsmen. In the meantime the craftsmen who are doing the outlining can't see their subject. Later in the video, similar ladies are depicted by outsiders whom they had met the earlier day. In only one single week, the video had accomplished in excess of 15 million perspectives from around the world. An article about the video was shared on Mashable multiple times within 24 hours. One primary motivation behind why the video performed so well was it depended on an amazing all-inclusive human truth which is something that each lady could identify with and get it. The substance was new, sincerely established, and did not feel like a promotion for the Dove magnificence item by any means.

In case you're an advertiser of a huge brand, you may have the dollars to put resources into some paid publicizing strategies. YouTube gives a few alternatives depending on your destinations. They arrange the destinations as Brand Awareness, Product Launch, Direct Response, and Reputation Management.

After you've decided your goal, you are offered advertisement positions including the following:

- Home-page promotions: This furnishes the sponsor with a debut spot on the YouTube landing page. In excess of 50 million exceptional clients go there consistently. It's prime promoting land.
- TrueView Videos advertisements: YouTube presented this promotion design a couple of years back that enables clients to click a Skip This Ad Now catch after the client has seen the promotion for five seconds. With this prominent organization, promoters are roused to make the initial five seconds of their recordings especially fascinating.
- Brand channel: This classification offers a few dimensions of customization for a channel committed to your image. The customizations incorporate how the page looks, what recordings are advanced and how clients are attracted to it. This is unique in relation to a client channel, which is free when you join.
- Mobile: Video promotions are served up on your client's cell phones iPhone, Android, and BlackBerry. Score records YouTube as the main goal for portable video.

SOCIAL MEDIA MARKETING AND PERSONAL BRANDING

With these paid strategies, YouTube furnishes all the standard media measurements with YouTube Insights. These incorporate impressions, snap to play, active clicking factor, and quartile saw notwithstanding the network measurements (likes, perspectives, and remarks). A quartile see demonstrates the information portioned in equivalent quarters with the goal that you can decide how well each is getting along. Additionally incorporated into the measurements are socioeconomics, areas of viewership, watcher sources (where the clients originated from to see the video), and the amount of the video they saw. These measurements are illuminating to the point that they are presently constraining promoters to reevaluate how they make recordings.

Llikewise, you can focus on these notices to keep running while you also select an accomplice content. This situation matters to numerous advertisers who stress over what their very own promotions (video or something else) may show up beside.

At the conclusion of this module, you should now have an improved grasp of how you can put your video marketing campaigns - if there are some - onto the YouTube platform. It takes a while to build up a significant following but if you do it right, you'll be a YouTube sensation before you know it.

Chapter 7

Pinterest

7.0 Introduction

Imagine that someone came to the virtual lobby of your business (or your real lobby) and offered to create a fabulous wall of your brand images and products. It would be colorful and contain clear labeling. The most exciting thing about this wall is that if you point at one of the images, you're taken to a screen that tells you more about the product and helps you buy it. That's an offer you wouldn't turn down. Well, that's what Pinterest offers your business — and it's free!

In March 2010, Pinterest launched its beta. It was met with polite applause from friends and colleagues of the startup. But not many people were understand how to use it. At the later year, it was listed in Time Magazine's 50 Best Websites of 2011. Omnicore Agency stated that as of September 2018, Pinterest has 250 million active users monthly, 50% of whom are outside of the United States. It now has over 3 billion boards and more than 175 billion pins.

For the uninitiated, a "pin" is anything and everything that a user uploads to their profiles - photos, videos, recipes, what-have-you. It's the *individual*, stand-alone content. Other users can then share this pin to their own profiles - what's also called "pinning". On the other hand, a board is a category - all similar pins can be lumped together in a board.

So going back - what caused this explosion of interest? The answer is visuals! It provided a fool-proof way for people to share pictures of things they liked and perhaps wanted to buy. Because of the ease with which users can post external links on their photos, it was just a quick hop from pinning pictures to a digital board to buying them online. According to the Social Intelligence Report Q4 2013 Adobe Digital Index, Pinterest's revenue per visit is up 244 percent year over year and 69 percent quarter over quarter. That's pretty an amazing growth!

To optimize your use of Pinterest as a business tool, you need to understand how members use it. If you are already a user, you're ahead of the game. If you have never used it, help yourself by exploring it first as a user would.

In this chapter, we look at how to get started with Pinterest, find interesting pins, collaborate with colleagues, distribute marketing materials, and sell products. You'll also have some fun along the way!

7.1 Recognizing Pinterest Users

As you know, visuals instantly attract your eye. Your brain understands them more quickly than the written word and is more likely to respond to them. Posts with images have a greater response on all the social networks.

To understand the attraction of Pinterest, you need look no further than the home page. It contains hundreds of images of things you personally like and respond to. How does it do this? Take a look at getting started with Pinterest and you'll see how social media marketing with Pinterest can attract new customers.

As a baseline, it's important to note that Pinterest users are approximately 70 percent female (majority of users between the ages of 25 and 44) and 30 percent male. If women are not your target audience, however, don't turn away just yet. You have several important reasons to consider Pinterest as a social media marketing tool:

1. **Large number of users**: As we said, Pinterest is growing every day. You have an active group of women (50 percent of whom have children) who are happy to re-pin. They wish to recommend items as well as buy for family members. We've also seen reports that men are starting to catch up and use Pinterest for organizing information like travel info and hobbies.

2. **Good distribution tool**: Sharing is the order of the day. You never know who will share something on your website. One person could pin your photo, and their connections will pin it from there, and the sharing train just continues!
3. **Easy sales tools**. Selling from the gift section is very easy; you just have to put a link to your store to redirect Pinterest users to the products on your website.
4. **Excellent showcase:** Based on the way the system is constructed clearly and and clean-cut way, almost every pin looks good. Why not take advantage of that?
5. **A lot of time spent pinning**. Because a user's homepage *only* has photos that they're interested in, they typically spend more than 15 minutes looking around. That's a long time to hold consumer attention.

Over the next few pages, we focus on Pinterest for business. If you want to familiarize yourself before signing up as a business, you can sign up with a personal account. It's easy to convert to a business account - it's literally just a click of a button!

7.2 Exploring the Interests of Users

To see topics of interest to you, Pinterest suggests that you choose five boards to start. When you begin, the site displays a text link at the top of your page that says, "Want to see more Pins you love in your feed? Follow interesting boards." Click that link and choose your topics.

Users have lots of other ways to find interesting pins. You may just type keywords into the search box and see what comes up. Another alternative is to click the button next to the search box with the lines on it (signifying a list). When you click this button, a window pops up, displaying all the categories you can choose your interests from.

One way to see what's hot on pinterest is to check out its "popular" board by clicking that category link. Going to this link shows you what people are currently pinning and may give you some ideas.

7.3 Pinning As A Social Activity

Pinterest makes finding and sharing pins a truly social activity. Previously it would have been a marketer's dream to have potential customers trading pictures of their products and commenting on them. Now, customers can go right to the source of the pin and buy the product.

Features like re-pinning, liking, and commenting create targeted groups with common interests who can also recommend your product to friends.

In the interconnectedness of social media platforms, it's important to make it easy for users to pin from whatever platform they're on. Download the following for your pinterest site to help your users out:

- **A pin widget for your website**: Having a website pin lets users pin anything on your site to their Pinterest account.

- **A board widget**: This widget lets you embed your favorite Pinterest board (displaying up to 30 pins) on your website so that visitors can see a representative sample. Your goal is to entice people who visit your website to go to your Pinterest account

7.3.1 Focusing on Strategy

Now that you've seen Pinterest through the eyes of a user, this section tells you about three key ways to use Pinterest to achieve your business goals:

1. **Use the power of visuals to attract followers**.

First and foremost, you need to think of Pinterest as a gigantic billboard for your company that can be seen by millions. Users can find images in all sorts of ways because they are pinned and re-pinned. You never know how many people you can reach until you start pinning and getting feedback. You can see what's popular and determine how to create more content of that type.

1. **Develop cross promotion**.

Cross promotion to and from Pinterest will power up your other marketing efforts and is the key to optimizing your use of Pinterest. Every one of your social media channels should provide the capability for users to pin items to Pinterest and then send them to other channels. For example, a user can pin from your website to Pinterest, and on Pinterest you can provide a link to your blog.

Or, say that you're planning a new marketing campaign that includes all sorts of exciting graphics and new pages. Make sure that all those items get pinned to a board that supports the campaign with the same discounts and promotions. With this strategy, you leverage what you've already created.

1. **Leverage your existing business strategy**.

Although leveraging your current business strategy might seem obvious, it is often overlooked. Because Pinterest is so different from other social networks, businesses hold it apart from their other business strategies. Actually, it is the perfect complement to any marketing plan. The key is to determine how it serves your current interests. As you develop a strategy for using Pinterest, remember to create hashtags that support your goals. Users can also use the hashtags they want, but don't leave it to chance if you have some strategic goals. For example, if you are planning a major conference and have developed hashtags, be sure to use them on your pins.

7.4 Becoming a Business Pinner

To get started with Pinterest for Business, go to http://business.pinterest.com/en and enter your email address or your Facebook login. Getting started is easy and free! After you have signed up and chosen your name, you can start creating boards of topics that interest you, and pin items to them.

Don't forget that if you want to pin to any of your boards from your mobile device, you need to download the iPhone app in the iTunes store or the Android app from Google Play.

7.4.1 Setting up your profile

In this section, you can explore how you might set your profile as business user. As a business user, you want to make your brand clear and understandable. This section looks at how two lifestyle companies list themselves on Pinterest. One uses a person as a brand, Martha Stewart, Inc.; the other, L.L.Bean, uses the company brand. Both do a great job of conveying what their brands have to offer, but they do it in different ways. By looking at each type, you can see what might work for you.

You don't have to be a giant conglomerate to succeed. Millions of people are enjoying and buying from small and midsize businesses, too.

When you sign up as a business, the profile sections for Pinterest boards are Name, Picture, Username, About You, Location, and Website. Here's what Martha Stewart and L.L. Bean do to communicate with customers.

7.4.2 Example profile: Martha Stewart (MS)

Martha Stewart, who is known for her beautiful presentations of food, crafts and home design, uses Pinterest to its full visual advantage. Her main website is http://www.marthastewart.com/.

- **Name**: In this case, the name "Martha Stewart Living" is used. She names her boards in a way that helps her bridge the gap between personal and business. Give some careful thought to the name you want to use to identify your company. If you are a "solopreneur" or small business owner you can use your name and, in the description, list the name of your business. It depends on how closely you are identified with your brand.

- **Picture**: The name you chose previously would dictate the picture you use for your profile. If your name and face are part of the brand, you use your own picture. If you're not, you use your logo. Even though some companies have a logo, they use their CEO's picture because that person has "celebrity" status. For Martha Stewart, you see her own picture.

- **Username**: This is the URL by which your site will be identified. For example, MS has https://www.pinterest.com/marthastewart/.

- **About You**: This descriptive content shows up beneath your name and serves as a description of you and your brand. Here's where MS incorporates both her personal boards and her company boards in the same place, for a total of a whopping 165 boards. Along with her boards Around, My Farm and My Pets, you also can connect to her departments for Living, Weddings, Crafts, and Products. The links take you to instructional information that has value for the reader.

The site has no hard sell and the text comes across in an authentic manner. The company focus is to be the authority on how to create a beautiful life so she mixes crafts with recipes, gardening and everything in between.

- **Location**: MS lists New York, NY, as where her business is located. Previously, it was listed as Kaitolah, where she actually has a home, not a business. You can opt to use either of these options for your own location.

- **Website**: MS links to her website (you must have your site verified by Pinterest). You can also link to Twitter and Facebook.

7.4.3 Example profile: LL Bean

The main page on Pinterest for L.L. Bean displays the following:

- **Name**: The company name used is L.L. Bean.

- **Picture**: The company logo, which is well known to users.

- **Username**: https://www.pinterest.com/llbean/

- **About You**: Asserting that this is the official pinterest site for L.L. Bean, this area says, "Welcome to the outside. The official Pinterest for L.L.Bean. #BeanOutsider". Their 32 boards focus totally on the outdoor user experience with LL Bean Products.

- **Location**: Freeport Maine.

- **Website**: Here you find a link to the official L.L. Bean website.

One interesting comparison is between L.L. Bean's weddings board and MS's wedding board. The brands clearly delineate themselves visually. L.L. Bean focuses on the outerwear and outdoor activities that wedding goers are experiencing. MS focuses on elegant fashion, flowers, and food. Think carefully about the visual statements you want to make, and never stay away from that focus.

7.4.4 Starting a group board

A group board is a board that several people can share and contribute to. The owner of the account simply need to invite people to add pins to the board by clicking Edit at the bottom of the board and choosing "Who can add pins". Once a user accepts, they can pin anything they want. This system works really well if you have several people on your team who need to supply marketing pins. It also allows you to add colleagues and vendors from outside your team. It's an efficient way to collaborate with everyone who needs to have access to the boards.

Don't be reluctant to add pinners if you need to. Anyone on the team can delete pinners and even block them if you have an issue. You won't be stuck with pinners if they leave or cause a problem.

7.4.5 Creating secret boards

Does the title grab your interest? Secret boards sound so mysterious. They are really a great tool for personal or business use. Secret boards are just what they sound like. They are boards that only you and your chosen friends can see; they aren't public. Imagine the possibilities for you and your collaborators! You can create projects and keep them under wraps. Then you can unveil them when you're ready or keep them permanently secret. How about a board for new product development or perhaps one for personal dream trips you'll take?

Pinterest found out that users liked secret boards when they allowed them to create three secret boards during the 2013 holiday season. After users got the hang of it, they found all sorts of ways to utilize them for holiday shopping lists, secret wish boards, and more. Because of the interest, Pinterest now lets you create up to 500 secret boards at any time. We doubt that you'll have that many secrets, but it's worth a try!

You can create a secret board by following these steps:

1. Log in to Pinterest.
2. Click your name in the upper-right corner
3. Choose your profile and pins
4. Scroll down to the bottom and click the plus sign to create a secret board
5. A window pops up asking to keep it secret - yes or no.

7.5 Developing credibility for your profile

This section explores the types of images that you should consider posting for your business.

Obviously, you want to choose images that are colorful and convey the essence of your brand. Pinterest has several kinds of pins that you can create, as follows:

- **Image pins**: JPGs or videos, which make up the majority of pins you see.

- **Promoted pins**: Pins you pay for.

- **Rich pins**: Allow you to add extra information that makes it easier for customers to find your pins. Use them liberally. You can include pins about movies, recipes, articles, products, and places.

If you want to create a map board, you can select the map option when you are setting up the board. Only the board owner can select the map option, so determine whether you will need it when you set up the board.

You can create as many boards as you need to communicate your message. Don't skimp, and don't worry about whether each one is perfect.

The key aspects of a board are its title and cover picture. These aspects are what the users see first. If the name and picture are straightforward but still enticing, users are likely to at least click to see the board. You have no guarantee that users will stay and perhaps even click other pins, but you want to at least get their attention by making a good first impression. Liken your board to a book cover and title. If your board's title and cover picture aren't immediately intriguing, users won't explore it.

Always encourage your audience to do the following:

- **Repin** your pins to get them circulated.

- **Comment**, because as you know the opinions of friends and colleagues are most valuable.

- **Share and use your hashtags** to let your customer be your best salesperson. Make sure your content is pinnable from your website using widgets.

- **Buy**, which is your favorite customer activity. Make it easy to click the buy button. Evaluate each pin for its usability.

7.6 Narrowing down with guided search

Pinterest wants to make it as easy as possible for you and your customers to find exactly what everyone is looking for. In 2014, the site introduced Pinterest Guided Search for iPhones, iPads, and Android. Guided Search is useful because it lets you to narrow down within a category.

For example, say that your customer is looking for plants for her shaded patio. First she types in shade and gets items including shade garden, shade plants, and shade flowers. She chooses shade plants. Then she is shown additional categories to pick from.

As a marketer, it is important that you conduct these searches for products on mobile devices. You want to know exactly what users will find and how you can make it easy to find your products first.

7.7 Tracking your results

It's easy to assume that your Pinterest traffic is converting customers. But perhaps it's not, and you need to know. You need to analyze what you're doing. Several tools are available to help you see what your customers are doing on Pinterest. These tools include:

- Pinterest's free **built-in analytics dashboard**: You can access this dashboard by first verifying your website and then clicking your account picture in the upper-right corner and choosing Analytics. You can track such items as how many pins are coming from your website in a certain timeframe, what users share most often, and what pins get clicked most.

- **Tailwind**: Tailwind has a free version of this tool that tells you, for example, which pins are being pinned from your website, your number of followers, and the number of re-pins. A professional version is available for a charge.

Chapter 8

Tumblr

8.0 Introduction

Which web-based life has around 456 million sites as of January 2019 and 520 million over a six-month length? If you guessed Tumblr, then, you are absolutely right. In 2014, Tumblr was purchased by Yahoo! for an uncovered 1.1 billion dollars. What started in 2007 as a way for David Karp, Tumblr creator, to easily post media changed into a visual powerhouse with an expansive number of customers.

What makes a Tumblr blog so captivating? It's definitely not hard to use and your image types look remarkable. Tumblr web diaries change from other online life locales since you aren't asked to fuse since quite a while prior, included substance posts. They are proposed to serve the photos that they show, and the interesting thing is bolstered. In this part, we look at what you need to do in any case Tumblr and how to parade your substance to its generally conspicuous advantage.

8.2 Setting Up Shop on Tumblr

Tumblr is free to join and is hosted for you on Tumblr's site. You don't have to worry about getting your own hosting site or paying for a suitable WordPress or other blogging template. This is not insignificant. You probably don't need to hire a developer at the beginning to help you set up your site. However, if you want to customize the template and develop special features that'll help your company, you'll want to consider some assistance.

So, who uses Tumblr? Statistics gives us some interesting demographics about Tumblr users. As of October 2018, about 33% of all desktop users are from the United States, with other 4 countries in the top 5 being the United Kingdom, Brazil, Canada, and Germany, respectively. In the United States alone, 44% of users fall into the 18-24 age bracket and 34% in the 25-34 age bracket.

8.2.1 Creating an account

Like most other social media platforms, creating an account on Tumblr only requires a few easy clicks of a button. All you need to do is think of a distinct URL and blog name that's going to set you and your brand apart. Obviously, you're going to want something that your customers can recognize, remember, and easily go back to. If you're lucky, the name and domain you want won't already be taken by someone else.

Once you have that set up and verified, you're good to go!

8.2.2 Creating the good stuff

You already have a grasp of the initial two things the next is you have to concentrate when putting up a latest platform on your campaigns in social media are the steps below:

1. **How it will become a big help with your customers.**

Are your clients as of now on Tumblr? Make a point to affirm this and see how your clients are utilizing it. On the off chance that you serve a youthful statistic, see to it to join the lively soul of other Tumblr online journals. In the event that your gathering of people fits the statistic however is somewhat more established, don't be hesitant to utilize your blog to flaunt your media. IBM works to the perfection of utilizing Tumblr to convey its message (look at it at (http://ibmblr.tumblr.com), by showing an assortment of classifications.

1. **How it will come along with your strategy.**

Your methodology must be the highlight of all that you do, and you have to lead your Tumblr in a way that incorporates this technique. In the event that a significant amount of share of your clients is not yet on Tumblr in any incredible numbers, you should think about utilizing it to improve your present conveyance — for instance, incorporate connections on your different channels to media on Tumblr.

It's most crucial to keep in mind that your Tumblr blog should not be a duplicate of the content you have on Facebook or Twitter. Tumblr gives you the privilege to include multimedia in a more efficient manner. One of the most useful aspects of having a Tumblr blog is that it forces you to think about more than just text. This is a good thing, since most business blogs are pretty dull and companies don't even realize it. You are challenged to break out the media you own or create something new.

With a Tumblr blog, you have no excuse for posting a few paragraphs and calling it a day. The world of visuals and multimedia is open to you. As a social media marketer, you can make this cornucopia of media choices work to your advantage. You can put up multimedia on Tumblr that's not on your other platforms and then link it. Just don't make your other platforms a "me, too" of Tumblr. Things will not work out for you that way.

To make it easy to select items to curate from your browser, you can also place a Bookmark in the menu. To do this, go to https://www.tumblr.com/app, and drag it onto your browser.

8.2.3 Finding and sharing the good stuff

Tumblr is primarily a community that both creates its own content and shares others'. As a marketer, you're going to want to amass as many followers as you can to get your content shared to as many people as possible. This starts with exploring the platform and all of the content that's related to your brand.

So how do you build your network on Tumblr? Here are a few ideas:

1. **Utilize the hashtags**: Like Twitter and Instagram, Tumblr uses hashtags to categorize its content. Experiment with what hashtags have a lot of related content to your brand. On

Tumblr, the more the tags, the merrier! The point is to get more people to see your content, and a lot of people use hashtags to find what interests them.
2. **Reblog whatever is relevant**: You can easily access related posts by clicking on the hashtags and sharing - or, using the appropriate terminology, "reblogging" - what's relevant to you. It also builds a relationship with the user who created the post so if you're reblogging, always give credit to the owner!
3. **Follow, follow, follow**: Exploring the hashtags can also lead you to other users who are posting similar content. Dig around their profile a little more and see if they seem likely to reblog your posts. If you follow them, they're likely to follow you right on back.
4. **Be consistent**: Having a Tumblr profile requires regular upkeep. You're likely to lose followers over time if you're not posting things regularly enough. One of the great features on Tumblr is the ability to schedule posts. You can have a whole lot of posts lined up and the platform will post them for you at the time intervals that you decide on.

8.3 Understanding your Tumblr activity

It is possible to integrate Google Analytics into your Tumblr page so you can track how many users visit your page, as well as other demographics. However, because of the way the Tumblr has structured interaction on their site, there are certain limitations in that, many people may not visit your Tumblr homepage, actually relying instead on what you post that comes up on their Dashboard (similar to the Newsfeed we see on Facebook).

Tumblr has its own built-in activity tracker, which you can view by clicking on the human silhouette on the upper right-hand corner of your browser page. When you look at the activity, it will show you a graph of followers and "notes" over a period of time of your liking.

Notes indicate any time that a user interacted with your content by either liking or reblogging it, or both. Unfortunately, the longest time period that you can track your activity over is a month, so partnering this with Google Analytics may still be the most insightful.

Chapter 9

Google+

9.0 Introduction

A couple of years prior, a part covering Google wouldn't have been required in a book via web-based networking media showcasing. But since Google has done as such much in a previous couple of years and has plans to do as such substantially more in the following, a section on Google is without a doubt currently justified.

Google+ propelled in June 2011. Brand pages were added to the platform in November of that year. Google made a social music administration and structured a Google catch for use on different sites and for incorporating different social highlights into Google Search. Apparently, Google's social desire is a lot more noteworthy than its substances today (Google+, for instance, has roughly 540 million clients contrasted with Facebook's billion or more clients), however, that doesn't mean the future may not appear to be unique.

In this part, we'll find how Google has changed from a straightforward web search tool to an internet-based life platform. The point is to have you see how to utilize it further bolstering your good fortune as an advertiser with the rules, tips, and traps.

9.1 Looking at Google's Social Strategy

To realize how to tackle the Google web biological system for online networking showcasing, you have to initially comprehend the center of Google's own social methodology. Generally, Google is as yet an inquiry platform and the most visited webpage on the Internet for both content-based pursuit and video. Most by far of Google's incomes and traffic, originates from Google Search. That is probably not going to change sooner rather than later. Be that as it may, throughout the most recent couple of years, the ascent of Facebook has truly compromised Google's online predominance. An ever-increasing number of individuals look to their companions on platforms, for example, Facebook when they're looking for data, regardless of whether it be item data or eatery suggestions, much of the time even before completing a Google seek. Therefore, Facebook has begun to strip away publicizing dollars that used to go to Google. This has ostensibly made Google anxious.

Google is reacting to this danger in two distinctive ways. To begin with, they've attempted over and again to make interpersonal organizations to rival Facebook, for example, Orkut, which took off just in Brazil and India, and after that Google Buzz, both of which have been shut down. It is fair to say that the Google strategy of creating competing social networks largely failed.

Now, there's Google+, which is designed less as a social network and more as a "social layer," which means that existing Google applications become more social when they are integrated with Google+. Google has decided to make every other part of the Google ecosystem more social through Google+. Whether it is Google Search or Google Music, Gmail, Google Maps, YouTube, or even Google Apps, they are all getting more and more social through their integration with Google+.

So how does this integration work? The Google+ profiles are used as the background account for many Google services. When you search on Google, you contents shared via Google+ profiles and brand pages. Both of these approaches present unique social media marketing opportunities for marketers.

9.2 Grasping the Google+ Fundamentals

Google+ is another kind of social network for anybody and everybody on the web. Founded in June 2011, on its surface appears to be fundamentally the same as Facebook. Notwithstanding, it does without a doubt have some engineering contrasts that have served to draw in clients to it.

Following are the most crucial features of it:

1. **Google Stream**: This is the landing page that you see when you sign in to Google+. It demonstrates to all of you the posts by individuals in your circles - your associations. Similarly as with Facebook, you can present a message on your stream. The message can be from your own record or a brand page. Be that as it may, even better, after you type the content (or transfer the photo or video), you can pick which circles or which individuals in those circles to impart substance to. In this design, you can firmly oversee who gets the opportunity to perceive what bits of your substance.

2. **Google+ Photos**: Google has put in some pictures that is more squeezed into its web infrastructure. Pressing the Google+ photos icon will bring you to a photo page that is pleasing to the eyes and very useful for everybody. The Google+ Photos philosophy is that the lens from which you view other people's photographs should be the same lens through which you view the content stream. On the Google+ Photos page, you can choose to view photos in the following categories: photos from your circles, photos from your phone, photos of you, photos from your posts, and your albums (integrating the Google Picasa application).

3. **Google+ Profiles**: Every user on Google+ has a profile page that is similar to the Facebook profile page. All your activity appears on it, including the pages that you may have "+'d" in the past. When you click the +1 button (known as the Google Plus One button) next to some content, you are sharing content with your Google circles. It's similar to the Like button on Facebook. You can select any kind of media (either your own or others') and let people know about it. You can add a photograph, share some information about yourself,

upload photographs and videos, and allow others to send you emails and messages from this page. The profile page also shows how many people are in your circles and how many circles you are in.

4. **Google Circles**: Integral to Google+ is the concept of circles, which is the categorization mechanism for people with whom you connect on the platform. They are groups of friends that you organize by topic. Topics can be as straightforward as friends, coworkers, and family, or as rarified as stamp collectors, Justin Bieber fans, and tennis players. On the Circles page, you can add friends to any number of circles. Then when viewing your news feed in Google+, you can limit the views by particular circles.

As you set yourself up in Google+, create professional circles of people who matter to you and your company. Whether from your personal account or from your Google+ brand page (more on that in the upcoming section "Google brand pages"), you want to create a circle for coworkers, influencers, competitors, and industry analysts. In fact, you could use the same categorization for your circles as your PR team does for its tracking documents. These circles help you keep track of what people are saying. Circles provide you with meaningful opportunities to develop relationships by participating in their conversations.

1. **Google+ Hangouts**: This is probably one of the more unique and fun features of Google+. Hangouts are like virtual rooms that let you run video chats with people who are in your circles. It is a focused video chat with friends, family, coworkers, or business contacts. Because Hangouts are triggered through circles; it is easy to find the group you want to talk to and then to set up a Google Hangout.

You can use Google Hangouts to have business conversations with other people in your company or even suppliers, business partners, or customers. If your brand is on Google+, Hangouts are a great way to socialize with customers or to run online events with them. For example, you can announce products on Google Hangouts and invite all your customers, business partners, suppliers, and employees to participate. Hangouts On-Air are particularly interesting because they give users the ability to create instant webcasts over Google+. These broadcasts can also be recorded for retrieval at a future date.

1. **Google+ Huddles**: Huddles, another valuable feature of Google+, enables you to run group messaging with people in a given circle. So just as Hangouts lets you run live video chat sessions with them, Huddles allows you to talk to them via group messaging. Google Huddles is currently available only for the iPhone and Android devices. You cannot access it from a web browser. Arguably, this tool has no direct implications for marketers as yet, but it is a useful collaboration tool among marketers within an organization.

9.3 Google Brand Pages

These pages are similar to the user pages on Google+ and include features such as Circles, streams, Hangouts, and Huddles, but they also have some key differences from those pages. The differences are designed to allow for the nuances of social media marketing as well as to prevent brands from over-marketing on the social media platform.

Following are the key differences with Google+ brand pages and what they mean for you:

- **Adding users to circles requires permission.**

A Google+ brand page cannot add a user to a circle unless that user has already added the page to one of his circles. This is very important because it prevents a brand from sending you messages until you have explicitly added the brand page to one of your circles and are open to receiving content from that brand. In other words, brands have to earn their place in a user's stream before they can start pushing messages into it.

- **Content is public.**

In contrast to personal profiles, pages on Google+ are set to public by default. This means that not only can the people who have the brand in a circle view the content, but anyone who visits the page can, too. Most brands want more people to see their content, so this default setting serves everyone well. It also gives individuals an opportunity to scan the content being published by the brand before choosing to add the page to one of his or her own circles. The default setting can be changed by the brand administrator.

- **Pages have +1 and Add to Circles buttons.**

Individual user pages have only the Add to Circles button in the top-right corner. Brand pages allow you to +1 the page or add content to it as well. The +1 button is something that Google is trying to push out across the entire Internet. When you +1 a piece of content, it improves that content's rankings in the Google search engine. And when you +1 a page on Google+, it brings about the same result as when you do so on an external website. This is a seemingly small feature but a very important one.

- **It is integrated with Search.**

Google is working hard to integrate Google+ with Google Search. If you search for a brand and add the plus sign (+) in the search box before the name of the brand, in the search results you'll be given the opportunity to add the page to a circle immediately. In fact, some users are taken directly to the Google+ brand page.

9.4 Tips and Tricks For Google+

Although Google+ may appear to be extremely large with 540 million users, many of those users do not use Google+ as a social network but just as a way to log in to Google services. We have yet to see how the platform will evolve and become really valuable for marketers. Only time will tell.

However, here are some tips and tricks to consider so that you are prepared for the many enhancements to Google+ that we know are coming:

1. **Set up shop on Google+ now.**

There's no question that the brands who set up shop early on Google+ are the ones who are able to attract the most people to their brands on the platform. This was the case with Facebook in its early days (some of the largest pages are still the oldest ones). The same applies to Google. In fact, we've already seen that the brands that were part of the Google+ launch already have significantly more people in their circles than the brands that joined later.

1. **"Write once, publish everywhere" doesn't work.**

Before you start publishing extensively on Google+, take the time to familiarize yourself with the platform and how individuals are using it. You'll notice that it is often used as a medium for more serious conversations. Although this may change in time, the threaded nature of conversations still remain with a more professional tone. As a result, don't automatically republish content designed for Facebook on Google+. You could, of course, repurpose the content and make it more suitable for the tone surrounding Google+

1. **Focus on search engine optimization.**

One of the hidden benefits of participating as a brand on Google+ is the search engine optimization advantages that come with it. Google+ is not a stand-alone social network. It is part of a broader Google ecosystem that has information discovery at its core. As a result, every link you post on Google+ as a brand that's then clicked as a +1 on Google+ gets better optimized for search engines. That alone is a compelling reason to be an early participant on Google+.

1. **The +1 that you see in Google+ requires attention.**

Not only do the +1 button clicks impact search engine results, but in time, they will also have a direct influence on paid search and display ads running on Google. If Google has its way, these buttons will be as pervasive across the Internet as the Facebook Like buttons. This means that when you redesign your website, you'll want to include those Google+ buttons. And even though having a brand page may not directly drive the increased usage of the button (that is, make your content and your brand be clicked as a +1 a lot more), having the community can certainly serve as a strong foundation.

9.5 Learning from the examples of others

The best way to learn what to do and what not to do on Google+ is to pay attention to what other brands are doing. See how often they post, what they post, and how their content sharing on Google+ jives with their Facebook strategies. Pay attention to user activity on their pages.

9.6 Listening to Google and Music

Just lately Google have founded a new feature in which it can compete with more well-known brands like iTunes on all kinds of devices. It is very crucial for Google to implement this so that their Android platform will not get left behind by Apple. In this section, we will discuss about the core service of it and its other features that will greatly help you in your social media marketing.

The Google Music has the following features:

- **You can upload all your songs to its platform.**

It can contain up to 20,000 songs without any fees at all. However, if you have a massive amount of songs, it can take a lot of time for it to be uploaded.

- **The songs can be utilized in various ways.**

You can manage your music on an Android device or through https://music.google.com/music/, too.

- **You can get a lot of song suggestions from it**

These suggestions are originated on what you possessed currently in the locker and the level of frequency you prefer. It also lets you purchase songs that will be on all platforms once you purchased them.

- **All the music that you buy in the Google Android Market can be shared.**

The most sought part of the Google Music platform is the feature of dissemination that you can enable. The way it works is simple: when you buy some music, you can choose to share it with your Google+ circles. After you've chosen which circles to share it with, your purchased content appears in their Google+ streams, where they can listen to the tracks for free (one listen per track). You can imagine that as the core Google+ functionality improves, the ways in which Google+ integrates with it also increase.

What does Google's entrance into social platforms mean for social media marketing? Just think about the possibilities for a moment. As a brand, you can not only share content with certain members of your customer base (through specific circles), but also potentially start sharing specific music. If you're a brand that plays in pop culture and for whose customers' music matters, this could be a really interesting way to attract attention to your brand and build loyalty around it. Needless to say, doing this right means doing it in a way that makes sense for your brand and for your customers.

Conclusion

When people start talking online, building relationships and meeting new people through people they already know, the simplest form of online networking begins. Just like the old word of mouth, inviting your friends who then invite their friend leads to an extensive networking circle. And with this came the social media expansion.

There is a difference between social networking and social media that needs to be made clear. Social networking is creating a web of connections between you and friends on sites such as Facebook, Twitter, LinkedIn, etc. Social media, on the other hand, is the content that you distribute. So it's about your content on blogs and all social sites. If you were to think about this in terms of coffee, the coffee cup or mug is the network. What you drink in it is the social media. If you decide to be, say, a cappuccino person or a latte person, would be up to you. In the same way online, you would do this by choosing your cup or network, which could be Facebook, LinkedIn, or any others. Then you decide what social media content (videos, pictures, text, etc) you will put inside it when you post, tweet, blog, or the like.

Although social media marketing seems to be fresh and new, it has been around for decades and actually goes back to the early days of computers and the internet. It may have been outdated and almost archaic before the world wide web (www) really took off with mass appeal, but it was still a method for online communication since the beginning of computers. Not so long ago, Friendster, MySpace, and Tribe, were coined as the innovative new sites until the likes of Facebook came along almost by accident. Founder of Facebook, Mark Zuckerberg, started his social network as a communication tool much like those before him, and he did so within his college campus to help students manage their social lives online. Hoffman, behind LinkedIn, seemingly suddenly emerged as well as one of the world's largest social networks. Most social sites started with different types of user-generated content, photo sharing, poking, and blogs among friends. But today, the Newsfeeds we see allow people to find out what is happening in their friends' circles, their businesses, and among colleagues' lives. All of this resulted in the biggest compilation of sharing information the world could imagine.

With new sites springing up all the time, millions of people are now able to turn to social networking sites every day to communicate with groups of people around them - in a sense of their community - about anything from informal announcements to important business news. Social media is a new modern media stream, aimed at social interaction with a selected target audience. Fantastic publishing tools give you the ability to reach friends and acquaintances through monologue type conversations which turn into dialogues amongst your fans and followers. More and more people are using social media to communicate. Different people use social media networks for different things. Some use it for PR, marketing, and broadcasting their business message to achieve a viral effort for a concept. Others use it for socialising and interaction within a community. Even freelancers, authors, and celebrities use social media networks to socialise with their fans. This goes to show the wide scope of social media and what it has to offer to you.

Traditionally, networking is about offering advice, doing favors and generally building business relationships which can be done online or offline. It can be a great way to promote your business and brand, and it offers a way to reach people who might otherwise be very difficult to engage by conventional sales methods. This progresses to a sense of personal relationships and potential clients.

With the deep dive, guidelines, and tips presented in this book for the top social media platforms available today, it's time for you to get started on your own social media marketing campaign. Good luck to you as you start the journey!

Personal Branding

The Best Strategies to Know How to Marketing Yourself, and Dominate Your Market .
By: Gary Clarke

Table of Contents

Introduction
Chapter 1: The Basics of Personal Branding
Chapter 2: How to Have the Right Mentality to Start Your Personal Brand
Chapter 3: What is Needed to Build Your Own Personal Brand
Chapter 4: The Steps You Need to Begin Your Personal Brand
Chapter 5: Remember to Be Yourself
Chapter 6: How to Choose Your Audience
Chapter 7: The Importance of Having a Mentor
Chapter 8: Why Do I Need a Good Team to Help Me Get Started
Chapter 9: Creating Your Personal Brand on Facebook
Chapter 10: Creating Your Personal Brand on Instagram
Chapter 11: Creating Your Personal Brand on YouTube
Chapter 12: Creating Your Personal Brand on Twitter
Chapter 13: Your Personal Brand Over Time – Tips to Getting the Most Out of Your Personal Brand!
Conclusion

Introduction

Congratulations on downloading *Personal Branding* and thank you for doing so.

The following chapters will discuss everything that you need to know in order to get started with your own personal branding. Just like working with branding a new product, or a company, a personal brand can help you to become more recognizable to a lot of people around you. Some people are looking to start with this personal branding in order to help them get recognized by their potential employer, and others want to start an online career and become a well-known personality. Either way, you will find that personal branding will be able to help you to get this done.

This guidebook is going to take some time to explore personal branding. We will look at what personal branding is all about, why the right mentality about tis process is so important from the start, the tools that you need to get started on your own personal brand, and some of the steps that you can take in order to get started with the personal branding process. Remember that this is not something that is going to happen overnight. But if you are able to follow the rules in this guidebook, and you are willing to put in the time and the effort, you will find that it can really help make a big difference in your life.

From here, we are going to take a look at some of the other things that you need to do in order to get started with personal branding. We will look at how you can put a good team together, how to pick out the audience you would like promote to, why you should consider having a mentor, and the importance of having a good team to help you get things done.

As we go through this guidebook, we will also explore the tips that you can use in order to promote your personal brand. There are a lot of social media sites that you can use in order to help you to see the best results. We will look at how you can do a personal brand with Facebook, Twitter, YouTube, and more.

Creating a personal brand is a great way for you to work on progressing your career, and many of your other goals. When you are ready to get started on creating your own personal brand in 2019, make sure to check out this guidebook to help you get started.

There are plenty of books on this subject on the market, thanks again for choosing this one! Every effort was made to ensure it is full of as much useful information as possible, please enjoy!

Chapter 1: The Basics of Personal Branding

At some point, you have probably at least heard the term of personal branding in the past. Whether you were reading a self-help book, heard it in the news, or you heard it at work, it seems like everyone is talking about having their own personal brand more and more nowadays. But this brings up the question, what is personal branding and why is it so important?

To keep it simple, a personal brand is going to be when an individual will make up their own titles and careers. And along with this, they will come up with their own personas and personalities to turn themselves into a brand. This can be a big concept that is hard to get a grasp of because it seems to be a bit ridiculous. You may be reading this and wondering, how can someone becomes a brand? Doesn't a brand need to be a product or a company?

When we take a closer look at what exactly a brand is, we are able to see why a personal brand can be something, something that can further an individual in their own career and life. Traditionally, a brand is going to be a uniquely named, uniquely designed entity that will be used in order to sell a single product or a chain of products. Brands will be used in order to sell the products and to make money, often because they successfully created an atmosphere that went with their name and their logo. If this is done in the right manner, these are going to be associated with a highly positive aspect of whatever is being sold.

Let's look at an example of how this is going to work. Most people at least know about the brand Nike, even if they don't personally use it. This company will produce a variety of athletic shoes and other clothing. Over the years, we have come to recognize their signature logo, and we know, without even seeing or hearing the name of the company, who Nike is just by that logo.

Nike has created that logo, and then placed it on every one of their products so that consumers know exactly who the brand is, and whether that is a product that they want to purchase. In addition, Nike doesn't just stop with the logo that they put on their products. They will take the time to endorse some of the famous athletes in order to create a wider branding image, even one that is going to be higher end than some of the others.

All of this, plus more, is going to be done in order to ensure there is an overall impression among the consumers when it comes to that particular brand. This is going to be evident as soon as you ask someone who would be a consumer of that product to summarize the brand with a few words. These could be things like performance enhancing, sleek, top of the line, and more. Or, you may hear that someone likes the product and thinks that Nike, and their line, is cool just because a certain celebrity has worn them.

The only difference between the branding that we just talked about, and personal branding, is that the branding isn't going to be done on a particular product, but it is going to be done for you. You will spend the time doing this same kind of branding on yourself, so that you can sell yourself to others, and get the things that you want.

Your personal brand is the look that you want to show to the rest of the world. You want to make sure that it comes off in a certain way, depending on the outlook that you are trying to get in the end.

Let's say that you are looking to get into a new position. You have finished college, or maybe even been in the field for some time. But now you have decided that it is time to take your skills and expertise and put it to the next level. You can easily work on personal branding in order to portray yourself in a certain way. To do this, you would craft your own persona through your resume, cover letter, emailing, social media sites and more.

You want to make sure that these are all cohesive throughout. This way, no matter how someone finds out about you, they are going to see the image that you want them to. For someone trying to advance themselves in the professional world, or someone who is just out of college trying to get their first career, you would most likely want to set up a personal brand that is professional, confident, and ready to do the job.

But personal branding an work in many other ways as well. You want to make sure that you know what your goal is before you start. If you want to grow your YouTube channel, your persona may be a bit different than the professional trying to grow their career for example. You have to know what you want right from the beginning, and then go for it by creating your own brand and showcasing that to everyone around you.

This guidebook is going to spend some time looking at the basics that you need to know to get started wit your own personal brand, especially in 2019. There are a lot of people who are trying to get the same customers, get the same jobs, and reach the same market. but there are only a few who are successful, and that is because they have mastered the art of personal branding and have done it in a successful manner. So, let's take a look at some of the different things that you can do to help start your own personal brand today.

Chapter 2: How to Have the Right Mentality to Start Your Personal Brand

Building your own personal brand can end up being a tough business. It is going to involve a lot of dedication and hard work, and it can take you some time to work on before you can even see the results. And if you are not in the right space mentally to do this work, personal branding can become even more difficult to handle.

Remember that this personal brand is meant to help you become more attractive, and more marketable, to the consumer. And because of this, you will be opening yourself up to the scorn of the public eye. And if you plan to make some profits from marketing yourself on Instagram and YouTube, you may find that you are going to be attacked by people you don't even know. If you have a consultant or a mentor who is helping you out, you may be reprimanded by them as you work with growing your brand.

You need to remember that it is so important to be in the right mindset from the very beginning. If you are able to do this, it is so much easier for you to make it through all of this, even if you were attacked or things weren't going the way that you would like. Some of the things that you can do to help make sure that your mentality is in the right place includes:

Be positive

When you first go into making your own personal brand, take the time to be positive. This is going to be hard. This is going to take time. and there are going to be some people who are not happy with what you are doing, and who will say mean things online. With all of this coming at you at once, it is important to remember to be positive.

Without this positivity, you will find that it is hard to keep going. It is easy to become really overwhelmed with all of the things that come with this branding. And if you allow yourself to get down with it, and not keep up the positivity, then it is hard for you to get it all done.

If you are worried about keeping up with your positivity, then start each day with the positivity that you need. You can start out with some good affirmations. You can choose to listen to some upbeat music. You can remind yourself of how it is going to feel when you finally reach your goals!

Be dedicated

Working on your own personal brand is not something that you can do part time. It isn't something that you can bring out when you have some free time, and hope that it is all going to work out for you. It isn't something that is always easy. Instead, you need to be able to dedicate your time to making this all happen. Creating your own personal brand takes time, and you need to be wiling to constantly work on updating it, improving it, and more.

If you are not able to spend at least a bit of time each day on making this personal brand, and you aren't willing to work hard to see the results, then you may as well stop now. Those who see the success that you are working for with this kind of branding, are the ones who understood how much dedication it takes.

The good news is, if you are passionate about your brand, and you are ready to make this personal brand grow your fortune and get you the fame that you want, this kind of dedication isn't going to be too hard. You may need to come up with a schedule to remind yourself of what to get done. This can help you to stay on track, even if you are busy with other things, like children, work, and school, you will still get the work done when it needs to get done.

Be passionate

Don't just put out some content just because you think it will get others to look at you. You need to be able to show passion to others about whatever you are showing off. Your personal brand can't just be some words on a page. Remember, there are a ton of other people who are trying to do the same thing that you are doing. And unless you want to be like most of them and you want to end up disappearing into nothing soon after you start, then you need to make sure that you are able to really make yourself stand out with something special.

Having a passion for your brand, even if it is a personal brand, and being able to show that passion in all of the stuff that you release to the public, will make a difference. Your consumer is smart. They know when you are actually passionate about something, or when you are just trying to put things up and trying to make money from them. Make sure that your passion is showing through; otherwise, it may be time to reconsider what you are doing since it won't bring you the passion that you want.

Be focused

When you are working on your own personal brand, you need to learn how to be focused. If you only work on the process every once in a while, if you spend too much time putting up random stuff that doesn't go together, and if you mess around and don't take all of this as seriously as it deserves, then you are going to run into trouble.

There are a lot of people out there who are trying to work with their own personal branding. This means that there is a lot of competition and noise out there. you need to be able to stand out from the crowd. And if you, and your campaign, doesn't have focus, this is something that will never happen. Learning how to focus your energy, and to keep your campaign working well can be the key that you need to help you to stand out and get others to notice you.

Be open to input

As you create your own personal brand, you will have a lot of learning to do. You won't know it all, and you may need the help of others to make sure that you are prepared and ready to take your brand to the next level. If you refuse to listen to any of the input that others give to you, then there is no way that you are going to be able to improve your brand, and you are more likely to fail.

This can be hard to do. There are always plenty of people who are willing to provide you with advice, and most of them have never done anything like this in the past, so they have no experience to help you. You have to be able to sort through all the noise and find the advice that is actually going to work for you, and not listen to everyone. This doesn't mean that you should avoid all advice and input though.

When you start posting about yourself online, and you work on your personal brand on places like YouTube, Instagram, Facebook, and more, you may find that everyone has an opinion. And most of these are not going to be the nicest. Many people have opinions about everything, even if they have no experience, and since they can hide behind a computer screen, they aren't afraid of sharing their opinion. This is probably not where you should get your advice from. Even if there are some good points hidden in the comments somewhere, it is likely that you are going to read a ton of negative, and not helpful, comments before that.

If you can, look for a mentor instead. Find someone who has worked on personal branding in the past, and then ask for their input. They may have some criticisms for you along the way as well. But at least this will be done as a way to make you more successful, not just a way to be mean. If you can find those who will be able to help you to promote your brand, and get the right persona out to others.

Have a purpose for all you do

When you are working on your personal brand, you need to make sure that everything has a purpose. You want it all to work well together. You don't want to go way off the path and turn others off from what you are doing with the rest of your work. You can't try things that are out of the norm, or things that don't' have a purpose, or you are going to turn others away from what you are doing.

This means that you will need to take some time to really think through all of the things that you post and put out there for others to see. It is fine to experiment a little and see if something works. But you need to think about everything that you are doing before you decide to let it out there. if it isn't going to work for promoting yourself, then it is time for you to make some changes.

When you are ready to work on your own personal brand, you need to make sure that you are in the right mentality. While there are a lot of different things that you are able to do to promote your own personal brand, you have to remember that there is going to be a lot of things that can go wrong. And with all of the people online, you will find that there are always people who will want to bring you down, who won't like what you are doing, and can say mean things along the way. Having the right mentality, and the right plan, from the beginning an make a big difference in the amount of success that you are going to see.

Chapter 3: What is Needed to Build Your Own Personal Brand

Now that we understand a bit more about this personal branding and what it is all about, it is time to build up the foundation for your own personal brand. This foundational work is going to eb something that you need to build up as time goes on, and in the long run, making changes and working hard on this personal brand will make a big difference in what you are able to do.

If you ever want to go on a career where you want to see success in the public eye, or one that is going to need you to have a good reputation with others, then finding a way to make your own personal brand is so important. Basically, personal branding is going to be essential for most professionals, although it is rarely used. The good news with this is that, since so few other people are doing this right now, you will have the upper hand.

Since this personal branding can be so important when it comes to what you can see with your personal success. Some of the things that you need in order to start building up your own brand will include:

Technology

Technology rules the world, and having a few basic components of technology can make a difference when you are creating your personal brand. First, you need to have a phone with you. And since you will need to be able to take calls, look up information, take pictures, download information to your social media sites, do live videos and more, it is probably best to aim for a smartphone. If you decide to keep a tablet on hand and use this for that purpose, then you may be able to get away with a simple phone, but most entrepreneurs like yourself will want the smartphone.

When picking out the smartphone, consider a few things. Look at how many pictures you can take on it, how sturdy it is (you will be taking it around with you on a regular basis so you want it to be able to stand the test of time). You can also look for a nice warranty to help you keep it in good shape as you move around.

Having some kind of computer will help as well. A laptop is a nice addition because it allows you to move around and do your work from where is the most convenient for you, but some people find that they prefer a desktop computer. Pick out the option that works the best for you. As you work on your personal brand, you are going to spend some time on this device, so going with one that is in good shape, and that has the right programming will make a big difference in the success that you gain.

Depending on the kind of thing that you are going to focus on with this endeavor, you may find that there are other options that you may need. Having a tablet is a must for some personal branders, as well as a good camera, good video camera, and more. Consider what you will need in order to get started and make sure you have the best to make this work better for you.

Knowledge about your topic of interest

No matter what industry you are trying to get into, you need to have a lot of knowledge to help you get started. there is a lot of competition out there for the consumer, and if you aren't knowledgeable about what you an bring to the table, then they will go with someone else.

Let's say that you are looking to get a job in the computer technology field. Would it make much sense for someone to hire you if you couldn't list off some of the basic programs that you can work with? Would they be likely to hire you if you weren't able to talk about computers, technology, and other similar topics? As someone who is trying to get the job, and why may be competing against a lot of other people who have more experience, you really need to sell yourself. And one way to do this is to know about the topic.

If you are able to come into that interview and talk about the topic, talk about some of the newest innovations with that topic, and get into a good conversation about it with the person interviewing you, it is more likely that they will take an interest. And if they are able to visit your social media sites, your own website if you have one, and look at your resume and cover letter and they all match up in showing your knowledge and interest about the topic, and shows your personal brand well, then you are more likely to get the job.

This can be true if you are trying to build up your own persona online as well. If you are trying to do a YouTube channel about building cars, you need to make sure that you are the best out there at making cars. You have to convince the consumer that you really know what you are talking about, that you are confident in your skills, and that it is worth their time to watch you, rather than someone else.

A good mindset

You talked about the idea of a good mindset earlier. If you start out on this process feeling down about yourself, or that it is not going to work out for you, then you will fail. But if you can come in with some positivity, with the determination and dedication to keep on moving, and some good goals in place, then you have the right mindset to make sure that you will be successful with this endeavor in no time.

Good social skills

It is impossible to make a good personal brand if you don't have the right social skills in place. Without these social skills, it is hard for you to meet new people, and form the connections that you need to see some results. Any time that you are building up a personal brand, and when you are trying to get that job, increase your reach on social media, or do any of your other goals, you are going to need to be able to build up some good social skills in the process.

There are a lot of things that you can work on when it comes to your social skills. Even if you feel shy or like you are not good with talking to others, this is something important to work on because it will ensure that you are able to reach your target market. To start with this, work on your eye contact. You will form a good connection with the other person if you are able to look them in the eyes when you are talking to them. This shows that you are truly interested in what they are telling you. If this seems awkward, look at their nose or just right below the eyes.

You can also mimic the other person a bit. This isn't meant for you to copy them and make fun of them. But make sure to watch how they hold themselves, how they move their hands, how they are standing, and how they talk. If you are then able to subtly follow these cues, you will get them to feel more at ease with you.

If you find that it is hard to get a good conversation started with the other person, then it is a good idea for you to come prepared with a few topics to get you going. This isn't meant for you to get stuck on a script. That will sound awkward and can make it difficult and stops the conversation in no time. Using these as guides, and then letting the conversation flow, can make a big difference though.

And finally, just go for it. Yes, it can be hard to network and talk to others. And yes there are times when you and the other person may not click and you don't get the response that is needed. But it is still important to get out there and make sure that you form some kind of connection with as many people as possible. Without good social skills, you will not be able to network and share information about your brand. Get out there, meet some new people, and remember that it is so important to socialize to increase your brand awareness.

Chapter 4: The Steps You Need to Begin Your Personal Brand

Now it is time to look at some of the steps that you need in order to ep build up that personal brand. Building this kind of brand can take some time. it isn't something that will happen to you overnight, and it definitely will not happen without some work ahead of time. but for those who are willing to put in the time, and give it their all, it can be a great thing, and will progress you in so many ways. When you are ready to learn more about creating your own personal brand, make sure to check out this guidebook to help you get started.

Identify what you have to offer others

No matter who you are, you are going to have some qualities that will make you unique. There is something that is special inside all of us, something that will make it so that others want to get to know us. Maybe it is your sense of humor, a winning smile. Maybe you are able to take a look at a situation and give some good advice to someone else. The positive aspects that come with your personality are going to be things that you need to focus on going forward when it comes to the personal brand you want to create. After all, personal branding has been described as selling the idea of a relationship with you to other people. With this in mind, you want to strive to sell the other people the best experience of you possible.

If you find that it is difficult to identify the best qualities that you can offer to other people, then it is time to enlist some help. You can talk to some family or friends, people who are looking to help you and who know you the best. Take a sampling of a few different people, ones who aren't too biased will be the best, in order to help you to figure out what unique personality traits and hobbies that you can bring to the table.

Remember, these good qualities don't have to just be things about your personality. You could include a lot of good things about yourself, no matter what area of your life they tend to come from. Everything has the some kind of value in what you bring to the table any time that you decide to make your own personal brand.

For example, maybe you are really good at color combination and wardrobe styling. Maybe you are good with programming and other things of technology. These are known as ancillary attributes. They won't be the main trait that you are trying to package into this personal brand, and they will not be the trade that you choose to capitalize on. However, these are less pronounced and smaller skills that are still really important and will be able to help you out along the way.

With this you will be able to come up wit your own little profile of yourself, one that you are able to use in order to further your brand. We are going to take a look at one of these as an example. Remember that you are allowed to write down as much as you would like, but in the end, you will need to come up with just one that you would like to focus on. It is great if you are able to make a nice list of all of these to showcase your strengths and your hobbies, but this can cause you to balance too many plates at once, and can make it hard for the consumer to follow you. Narrowing it down a bit can make a big difference. Some of the things that you may write down about yourself (but you can only choose one in each category) includes:

Personally traits:

1. Maybe a personality trait is going to be funny. You notice that you are able to make a lot of the people around you laugh on a regular basis, and it make you feel good that you can make other people laugh.
2. Informed. This could be a trait if you are someone who is always researching the current events around them, and trying to figure out which side of the argument is the best.
3. Creative: You may see this one as a personality trait because you are able to see things in multiple different ways. You may

be able to turn nothing into something, in a way that others just can't manage to do.

Ancillary skills:

1. Good with speaking in speaking.
2. Crafty. You like to build things, and you like to spend your time working on something new.
3. Technology.

With these things in mind, it is possible that you can come up with a few possibilities for how you are able to sell yourself, and this can make up your own personal brand. Maybe you would be able to teach, creating a variety of videos, books, and blogs about a topic. Maybe you could become a public voice or do some kind of talking, like a podcast. Along with the crafty part, you could use crafts and sell them on platforms and make money in that manner as well.

Once you have been able to go through and come up with your profile qualities, it is time to move on to the next step and research some of the options that you have for personal branding.

Research the types of personal brands, and then pick one out.

There are going to be different types of personal branding that you are able to pick out. And the one that you choose to go with is going to depend on the specific goals that you are looking to achieve. The most common form, and the one that is the easiest to work with, is going to be known as interpersonal branding.

When you are working with interpersonal branding, you are going to curate a persona, along with social media accounts, for the people in your personal life, such as your family and your friends. While this may sound a little bit deceptive, it is just a bit more concentrated effort to do what we have been taught to do since we were born. We do not say certain things to others because of how it may make us look, we do not flaunt or open up about our flaws until we get to know others well.

Basically, you will find that interpersonal branding is just going to take those natural tendencies that we have one step further and giving our social lives more attention. This may mean that you go through the social media accounts that you have, and polishing them up a bit. You can choose to give them a theme that is cohesive, and make them look more professional.

The next kind of personal branding that you can work with is going to be known as professional persona branding. This is going to be a branding type where a person wishes to take their professional set of skills, and then self-package it along with their professional skills so that they can seem more desirable to current and potential employers.

When you decide that it is time to create your own professional personal brand, you would either change your personal social media sites, or create a new one, and add in some more professional content compared to what you would have done in the past.

When you are working with this kind of branding, you have to pay attention to who would actually come to the social media platform to look at you. If you are trying to further your own career, or you are interested in impressing some of the people who are calling you for interviews in your own industry, then the professional personal branding is the right option for you. But you need to make sure that the information they see, the information that they are in contact with, will need to be professional, on target, and not include any gossip or other issues in the way.

Then you can move to the highest level of personal branding. This is what a lot of people are going to think about when they ear the term personal branding. The other two options that we talked about before will fall under this as well.

Personal branding, when we look at it in its fullest form, is when you are going to package together your skills set, social accounts, aesthetic, name, face, and personality and then you market it towards the public eye. This one is going to take some time and a lot of effort, but, if you are able to do it in a successful manner, you will be able to get the most benefits.

Many people who decide to turn their whole lives around and make that into a brand are the ones who would like to be in the public eye. This can be online or through some of the other media outlets that are available. And to be successful with this, you need to be willing to create a lot of content that is entertaining, creative and innovative, especially since you are competing with others who want the same goas, and you are trying to make yourself stand out.

So, from here you need to take some time and figure out which of the persona branding types you would like to work with. Do you want to just be socially seen in one way or another? Do you want to make sure that you are going to impress a current or potential employer wit your information? Or would you like to change up everything, and make your own persona for others to find online, and so that you can figure out new ways to create your own wealth.

Set your goals

Never start on your own personal brand without having some goals in mind. It may seem like a great idea to just run in head first and see what happens, but everyone who has tried to do that has failed in the long run. You have a lot of competition out there, and if you go in without any goals, and no idea on how far you should be, and at what point, it is going to be almost impossible for you to see the results that you want.

Before you get too far into this process, sit back and consider where you would like to go. What would success look like for you? Write that down, and then see if you are able to break it down into some smaller pieces. Working just towards one big goal, without separating it out into some little goals, can create a big mess. You will get worn out before long, and not feel like you accomplished anything in the process.

After you break down the little goals, you can start writing out a schedule of when you would like these to be done. Be reasonable here.

You don't want to set the deadline for so far in the future that there is no motivation for you to work hard and get them done. But you also don't want to set them so close that there is no chance. Maybe set the first few goals and see how that goes, and then adjust the rest of the goals from there.

As you accomplish each goal, you will be able to celebrate a little bit. It is a big accomplishment just working on your own personal branding, and it is something that can take some time and effort in order to accomplish. you should stop and take some time to celebrate all of the hard work that you have put in so far each time you reach a new goal.

Figure out who your audience will be

The next thing that you need to consider when you are trying to get started with your own personal brand is trying to figure out who the target audience will be. You are not going to be able to reach everyone with all of your message. There are just too many people out there, and this can waste a lot of time, money, and talents. Figuring out who your audience members will be can make a world of difference.

For example, if you are trying to make yourself into a YouTube star, your personal brand would look a bit different compared to someone who just left college and is trying to entice some of the employers that they applied with to look at their information. You would not want to waste your time and set up the same kind of campaign to handle bot of these.

Knowing your audience is going to make the process of personal branding so much easier than before. It will help you to know what kind of content you should write, what should be in the content, and even the different media sources that you should use. Make sure that right from the beginning you sit down and come up with the perfect target audience. This doesn't have to be difficult. Just think about who you would like to see this information once you are done with it.

You may find that you need to write this information out a bit before you get started. You can write out the words about the kind of personality or audience that you would like to work with. Or you can consider trying to write out a story about this person and some of their likes or dislikes are. You can keep this near you. It will ensure that you are able to keep your information on target, and that all of the parts of the campaign will stick together.

Find your team

Now one is able to create this kind of personal brand all on their own, no matter how much they may wish so. You are going to need a team of people who are able to support and to guide you trough all of this process. Those who will help you emotionally as you get started with this could include people from your family, or your friends. You could find a team who will help you gain the necessary resources, and who are able to invest with their time or financially to ensure that you are able to launch your brand.

There are a lot of different things that can go on when you are trying to create your own personal brand. Doing it alone just adds in a lot of extra work that you are not really supposed to handle on your own. Having people who can support you emotionally and financially, and having those who can bounce your ideas from and answer your questions, will ensure that your new brand can get off the ground.

Gather the resources that you need

The resources that we are talking about here will include anything that you are able to use in order to further your brand, and to help you reach your goals. The common thoughts on this right now includes three main types of resources, including treasure, talent and your time.

Your time is going to be any tie that you and your team will have in investing in your new personal brand. In order to figure out the type of time investment that you are able to make (because no one is able to work on this nonstop 24/7, you need to look at your current lifestyle and how much time you are able to give to this, and the availability of your team members as well.

If you are currently working a job that is from 9 to 5 each day, and you still plan to launch a personal brand, then you may find that more treasure or talent will be needed to make this a reality, because you may not be able to invest as time into it. And since you already went through and took stock of this resource before the process, you should have a pretty good idea of how much time you can invest into the whole process.

And when you decide to evaluate the treasure, you need to include material possessions along with your money. Things like the technology that you took the time to invest in, the software that you purchased, and even the clothes that you will wear can all come in and contribute to your personal brand.

Remember that investing your own wealth can add to the risk, and it certainly is riskier than investing your talent or your time. if you fail with tis process because you did not put in the work, it is possible to walk away form all of this with the talent in hand. And you are provided with some more time each day of the week. But your wealth is an investment that you are not able to get back ever. So, if you are going to invest a lot of money into this process, take the time to make sure that you are investing that money in the right way, in the manner that will make you feel comfortable and won't be adding in more risk than is necessary.

Begin to pour the foundation

When you have gotten this far, you should have been able to identify the thing that you are able to offer to the world. You will have a good idea of the type of personal branding that you would like to pursue, and you should have gone through and set up some new goals for yourself to help you get there. and this is just the start!

Once you are here, it is time for you to start the tangible work of creating your own personal brand. This means that you will need to go in and do the actual work of hanging your social media accounts, dressing in the wardrobe that you chose, creating content for your target audience, and basically just doing the steps that we talked about above for your own personal branding.

The steps that you do here are going to vary based on your overall goals with this personal branding, and what you would ike to see happen. Maybe you will spend some time taking pictures and videos that you are able to upload. You may go through and upload a few pictures to YouTube to showcase your products or some of your message. You may take any step that is necessary in order to get that new persona up and running, which can make it easier to sell it across all of the different platforms that you want.

Creating your own personal brand is something that can take some time, and some effort. It is not always as easy as it may seem, and lots of people have spent a lot of time trying to do for themselves. Creating a personal brand, whether you are doing it for personal reasons, professional reasons, and even for becoming more popular and like a celebrity, you will find that these steps will help you to get started in no time!

Chapter 5: Remember to Be Yourself

When you are working on your own personal brand, you will want to make sure that you are always yourself. It is sometimes hard to at like yourself when you start to post online. You may be worried about what others think about you. You may want to come off as cooler, or funnier, or something else when you work on this personal branding.

When you are trying to make up your new persona, and you are trying to get other consumers to like you, it is easy to try too hard sometimes. Or you may find that you see some negative comments come up on your page and you then decide to change up everything about yourself in order to try to change the opinions and make sure that you are more likeable to others.

However, even when you are trying to create your own persona, you need to make sure that you are still acting like yourself. This is one of the best ways to impress those who are watching your content, and will ensure that you are able to get the best results with your personal brand. People can see right through something that is fake, so don't waste your time, or their time either.

Since you are creating your own personal brand it is sometimes hard to remember that you can be yourself. But if you want to avoid the risk of turning others away from you and losing your target audience, then this is one of the most important things that you are able to do for your business. Let's take a look at a few of the things that you are able to do to ensure that you can be yourself, even when you are working on a personal brand.

Make your own hobbies a part of your brand

Whether you have a love for a certain sports team, you like to read, you like to fish, or your interest is less common, you can definitely use your hobbies in your personal brand. In fact, adding these in and talking about them, at least on occasion, is a great way to add some new life to your brand, and will ensure that it can stand out from the crowd.

Adding in these hobbies and interest will go a long way when it comes to making you more interesting and more genuine. And this is a great way for you to find a way to bond with your prospects and your clients who have interests that are similar to yours.

Show off the family

You don't need to show off every detail about your family to make this one happen. But if you are married and you have kids, or even if you are just married, then they are going to be a big part of your life. You should consider making them a part of your personal brand. You can do this by adding pictures of them on your social media accounts, and talking about them. There are a lot of ways to do this naturally, and it can really make a difference in the amount of connection that you can form with those around you.

Don't be shy

Even if you are a shy person in real life, it is important that you take the time to be a bit more outgoing when promoting your own personal brand. You need to really show others your true self so that they can start to know you and want to follow you. Even someone who is shy has a lot of other aspects about them. You just need to be willing to jump over that hurdle of being shy and make sure that you are showing these sides.

You will find that it is much easier to be engaging and interesting when you get over the hurdle of being shy. Even those who are really shy have something of value that they are able to give to those around them. This is a great thing to get you out of your shell as well. You have no chance of getting the results that you want and building up a personal brand, if you still stay shy.

The good news is that it is possible for you to be more outgoing, without even needing to talk to anyone else. A lot of the ways that we can build up a business in this modern world is online. If you do a YouTube video, you may have to get out of your shell a bit more to really impress the consumer because they are seeing you face to face. But if you write a blog, or try to promote things on your social media account, you will be able to reach out to that potential customer through the words you write, rather than talking to them in person. This alone should make it so much easier for even the shy person to step in and see some results.

No matter what though, you need to make sure that your real personality has some room to come out and shine. You do not want to end up with a lot of people turning away because you hide things, or you are too nervous to actually talk about what you want.

Act like your consumers are your best friends

When you are posting anything online, such as on social media, when you make a YouTube video, or when you write in your blog, one way to make sure that you are really showing off your good side, and your true self, is to pretend that the reader is your best friend. Pretend that you have known them for years, and that you both share a lot of secrets and fun times and laughter together through the years.

When you put a face to the audience, and you see them as friends, it is easier to be open and honest with them. It takes away some of the nerves that you are feeling, and makes it easier to work with them, to tell them more about you, and to drop the act of being fake and trying to impress them.

If it helps, write out a description of who you are talking to when you do this process. You can write a little backstory about them, their name, what they look like, and how you would like to talk with them. You can even put up a picture of one of your current best friends and pretend that you are writing the posts and01 the blogs and more in order to make it easier when you write.

Don't be fake

There are countless social media accounts out there that include people who just aren't able to be themselves. You take a look at them, and after just a few posts, or a few pictures, you know that they are just fake and full of themselves. These people have the perfect hair all the time, the perfect bodies, perfect families, and perfect life. You read through the information, and there is never one complaint to worry about at all.

While it is always a good thing to count our blessings and to be thankful for what we have, even when there may be some bad things going on, it is important to note that you shouldn't come off as fake. There is something as too perfect, even when you are on social media, and your audience is going to be able to spot this from a mile away. You have probably gone through a few of these profiles and thought how there is nothing substantial there, and that this person isn't really sharing the real them at all. This is a big turn off to many people in your audience.

Sure, you don't need to spend all of your time bashing those in your life and complaining that nothing seems to go your way. this is going to backfire against you as well and can turn a lot of your audience away. There needs to be a good balance here. Showing some of your vulnerabilities, like how you are human too, and how you do go through some struggles at the same time as well, can make a big difference in how people respond to you.

This again goes back to the marketing plan that you come up with for your brand. How do you want people to perceive you, and what kinds of posts are you going to put up in order to help you to accomplish this? If you decide to plan out some of your posts ahead of time, then you will be able to plan it out so you can have some real life posts, some humorous ones, some that are going to be informative, and some where you show the good things in your life.

Try to keep the drama at home

While you are supposed to spend some time working on showing your true self, you do need to filter it at least a little bit. You do not need to tell your consumer every little thing about yourself. There are some things that you want to leave at home. And this includes all of the drama, and much of the bad stuff.

When you are showing little parts about your personal life, remember that it needs to match up to the brand that you are trying to create. If it doesn't, then there is no reason to bring it out. Talking about a fight that you just got done having with your spouse is just going to seem petty and mean. And it is going to turn a lot of people off from you, especially if it just happened and the emotions are raw, and you are mad.

However, there is a way that you can use this to your advantage. Maybe you write a blog about parenting or relationships. While you don't want to go on social media and blast your partner right after the fight, you could take the lessens that you learn from that fight, and maybe write a blog about it. You can add in the personal details a bit (but not so much that it looks like you are just trying to get attention), to help prove your point or show the readers how you were able to get trough it. Of course, if you are working on a finance blog or a cooking blog or something that has nothing to do with the fight that you and your spouse just had, then eave that drama at home.

The image that you give out to others is important. Everything that you showcase on your blog, your social media accounts, and more, needs to match up with the brand that you are trying to sell. If it doesn't, then leave that information at home. But, no matter what kind of personal brand you are trying to create, you may find that adding in a personal touch, and showing your audience the real you will make a world of difference. It makes you seem more in touch with them, shows them something that is unique, and can make it easier for them to connect to you. Just make sure that you pick out stories, interests, and other things to share that are going to progress your brand, not ones that are going to put you in a bad light and turns others away from you.

Chapter 6: How to Choose Your Audience

Before you get too into making your personal brand, you need to take some time to really know your audience. It is impossible to market yourself to everyone. It would be nice if we were able to do that, but everyone throughout the whole country, no matter what the age, gender, job type and more, are not all going to like the same things. Know who will enjoy your information the most, and then putting your marketing efforts towards that will make a big difference in how well you turn your material to fit them, and how much money you can actually make with this.

Think of it this way. Person A is going to start a blog about parenting. They will most likely want to look for an audience who is about to have children, or who already have children, and who would like to have some advice about things that they are dealing with. They will look for mostly moms, and maybe some dads, with younger children. And they may choose to go with people who are a certain age, and in a certain location as well.

Then we move to Person B. This person is looking to get a job in accounting and wants to make a personal brand based on getting this job. They are not likely to want the same audience as what Person A wants because stay at home mothers are not going to hire them for an accounting job. They are going to look for employers who will hire them and will make that their target audience.

So, because there are so many different people throughout the world, and they all have different needs that should be met, you need to be able to come up with your own target audience to ensure that you can reach them, and that you provide them with information and content that they want.

This is going to vary depending on the audience that you want to reach and the topic that you want to focus your branding on. But no matter what your personal brand is about, there are a few things that you can consider when you are trying to pick out your target audience. These things will include:

1. What age they are. Usually this is going to be an age range, rather than an exact age that you will use. For example, you may decide that your target age range is going to be 25 to 35.
2. Gender: In some cases, you may find that you will go with male and female, but then other times, you may just want to go with one gender over the other. Decide which one works the best for what you want to accomplish.
3. Do they have a family? Does your target audience have a spouse, children, or other family members that are important to them?
4. Where do they work. The profession that the target audience has is going to influence their thoughts, hobbies and more so this is something that you should consider before you move forward.
5. What do they like to do in their free time understanding the hobbies of your target can help you determine if they are interested in what you are writing about. You should consider if you are able to make content that goes towards this or not.
6. Where they live. Knowing where the target audience lives is going to make a big difference as well. People are often going to respond in different ways based on where they live and what they are accustomed to.

These are just a few of the things that you need to consider when you are picking out your personal branding technique. There are a lot of different aspects that you can consider, based on the topic and theme that you are basing your personal brand on. Make sure that you are working to create a cohesive look to your personal brand so you can get the best results here.

One good activity that you can do here to make it easier to pick out your target audience is to write out what you imagine the perfect target audience member will be. Think about who they are, if they are male or female, what they look like, how old they are, what they do for a job, the things that they like to do for fun, whether they have a family, if they like to travel for work, and more. Write down a backstory to go with the target audience as well if you find that this is the best way to get that person stuck in your head.

Once this is done, you will need to keep this paper around. Place it somewhere that you will be able to get to easily any time that you write out a blog post, or you post in social media, or do anything else with your brand. Think about whether this message will speak to your target audience or not. Think abut what would impress them, and what they would like to hear. Then, use that to help direct your messages so that you stay on track, and you really work to build up your personal brand.

Chapter 7: The Importance of Having a Mentor

Another thing that you should consider when you get started with having your own personal brand is a mentor. Going it alone, especially with all of the competition that is out there and all of the noise that you have to fight against, can make this even more challenging. If you are able to find a mentor to work with you on all of this, someone who is going to guide you, give you advice, tell you when something is working and when it doesn't, and point you in the right direction, will give you a leg up on the competition and will ensure that you will actually be successful when you start your persona brand.

So, how do you go about finding the mentor you would like to work with? Look in your industry. You want to be able, if you can, find someone who has experience with personal branding in your own industry or your own niche. These individuals will have the specific experience that you are looking for, which makes them a goldmine of information to help you. They can walk you trough the exact process that they did, and if you do it the right way, you will be able to see the success as well.

Of course, you may not be able to find someone who is in your niche. This is especially true if you are working on a new niche or one that hasn't been done very much. Or maybe you just can't find someone who is interested. There are still other places you can look in order to find the mentor you would like to work with.

You may find that talking to someone who has done personal branding in a completely different niche. Or even talking with someone who has done branding for another business before. This may not give you quite the same insights as you would find when you are working with a mentor in your own niche, but it can make a big difference. They can still offer you a lot of the advice and tips on how to make your strategy better than ever.

At this point, you may want to figure out how to get someone to agree to be your mentor. First, you need to ask them. If you don't ask someone to be your mentor, how are they going to know that you need their help? You may be surprised at how many people, once you flatter them a bit, and explain that you think they are successful enough that you want them to be your mentor, will be more than happy to step up and help you out.

Using a bit of flattery in here can help as well. And showing them how it will benefit them, rather than just having all of the benefits go straight to you, will make a difference as well. Remember, these people have spent a lot of time working with their own personal brand up to this point, and they need to keep working hard to maintain it. They need to be able to see the benefit of doing this as well.

Some of these mentors will be happy to help out someone else because of the flattery, and because of you just asking. But if you are able to sweeten the pot a bit, and offer them something in exchange for their time, then that is a good thing to work on as well. You can consider giving them some recognition on your bog, mention them to your followers, once you get those built up a bit. Get creative here. Depending on who you decide to work with, there could be quite a few others who are talking to this person as well, and you want to be able to offer something that is different and unique.

Once you have been able to get the mentor to agree to work with you for some time, it is important that you don't waste their time. they are busy as well, and you don't want to end up with spending hours with them and not getting anything done. Before you meet up with them for the first time, after they have agreed to help you in the role of a mentor, you should take the time to write down the questions that you have. bring some examples of your blog posts, or your social media posts, and show them what you plan to do.

The more prepared that you can be for this meeting, the better it is for the both of you. When you have all of this information together and ready to go, you will find that it is easier for the mentor to provide you with advice, suggestions, and answers along the way. if you show up with nothing prepared, you just won't get as much out of the meeting as you really could.

If you are able to, try to set up the mentor relationship so that you can meet with them more than one time. there are a lot of things that are going to grow and develop with your personal brand over the years. Just getting advice at the beginning, and never double checking later on, will make it hard for you to grow over time. It is much better for you to spend your time meeting up with the mentor on occasion, even if it is just every few months, or a few times a year.

This is a hard thing to do sometimes. You and your mentor are often going to be busy, and finding times to do this together can be hard. But if you are prepared to work on your personal brand, and you want to be able to really make sure that you can get ahead, then this is something that you need to make important in your life and make sure that you are able to get the most out of these meetings.

During this time, remember that your mentor may not always tell you what you want to hear. There are times when they are going to talk to you, and tell you that you are doing something wrong, or that you need to go trough and change things up. Don't take this in a personal way. You wanted the mentor to make sure that you are able to get the most out of your personal brand. This means that if you do something wrong, you want to make sure that you get it fixed as soon as possible.

Yes, you may have worked hard on something for a long period of time, and are proud of the work that you did. And yes, it may mean that you will need to redo the work on occasion. But isn't it much better to hear about the stuff that you are doing wrong now, before you let it go on too long and drive away the customers and your personal branding goes out the window.

Having a mentor can be one of the best things that you can do when you are working on your personal brand. They will be able to tell you what is working, and what isn't working, so that you can do the best for your personal brand.

Chapter 8: Why Do I Need a Good Team to Help Me Get Started

If you are just working on making a personal brand in order to get that job that you have had your eye on for some time, then you will probably be able to do all of this branding on your own. You are just trying to gain a good reputation amongst a small market, and you will find that your employer will see you if you put in some time.

But if you are trying to grow a personal brand in order to sell something, or to promote yourself in a blog, videos, or some other way, then it is likely that you will need to reach a much bigger audience than you would have had to do in the past. Because of this, it is likely that you will need to take some time to find a good team to help you get started.

There is a lot of work that is going to go into turning that personal branding into something that is successful. It takes some time, and many times you are not able to do all of the work on your own. Working with a team, even if it ends up being just one or two people, will make a difference in how successful you are in the future. Some of the people that you should consider adding to your team will include:

Camera crew

The camera crew is going to be something to consider if you would like to create some high-quality videos. Remember that on YouTube, there are a lot of videos already present there. if you are building up your personal brand, you won't stand a chance if your videos look bad, the listener is not able to hear you, or there is something else that is low-quality about the video.

If you are just posting a few quick videos on some of the other social media sites that you are on, then you can probably do them yourself and your smartphone may be just fine. But many people find that a great way to build up the personal brand that they have is to work on some short video series on YouTube, and other platforms.

For those who are going with this second option, you need to find a way to stand out form the crowd. And having some high-quality videos, ones that are professionally done, will help you brand get the recognition that it needs, much faster than anything else. And it is unlikely that you will be able to do this all on your own.

Hiring at least one person, and maybe a crew, of people who know how to work with this kind of thing, and who will be able to walk you trough it all, capture the videos, do the editing, and upload it all in a professional manner, will make a big difference in the amount of success that you are likely to see. Don't believe that this is true? Try doing one video that is higher quality, and one that is lower quality and see how the views are different. Or find a low quality video on YouTube and monitor your own reaction to it.

Wardrobe

If you plan on doing a lot of videos on YouTube, then you may find that hiring someone to help you wit your wardrobe will make a big difference. This may seem like a silly thing to work on, but it is going to take a big difference in how well you are going to do. People, hopefully a lot of them, are going to see your videos, and you want to make sure that you come across as professional, and looking good in the process.

This one is not as important if you are working with other forms of promoting your personal brand. But if you plan to do a lot of pictures or a lot of videos, it may be worth your time to talk to someone about your style choices, and have someone, even if it is a friend who is good at designing or style, come in and discuss it with you. You want to make sure that you are really impressing the people who are going to watch your videos, and the outfits you wear, as well as the information you present and the way you present it, will make a difference in how they perceive you.

Marketing

At some point, you will hopefully be able to get your personal brand up and running to a point where you will see some tremendous results. But even in the beginning, you may find that a little bit of marketing can go a long way. marketing will ensure that you are able to reach the right target audience, no matter where they are, and it ensures that your message will get right out there to them.

Marketing can be hard to do, especially for those who are not really well-versed in making it happen. If you have never done this marketing in the past, and if you aren't sure about the first place to start, then it may be a good idea to have someone who does know about this take control for you. This can ensure that you will be able to reach the right people, at the right time.

The nice thing about having a person who is good at marketing, and who has done this in the past, is they can take all of the individual parts you have been working on, and bring them altogether. If you have a Facebook account, a blog, and Instagram account, and some videos on YouTube, then a good marketer is able to put together all of these parts, and ensure that they are cohesive, and that they can work together to make each one more powerful.

You can certainly try to do some of this on your own if you want. And it may be able to save you some money in the process as well. But this takes time, and learning the marketing system of each individual part of the process (such as how to do Facebook marketing and Instagram marketing) can take a lot of time. Having a professional will make a big difference.

Social media

Many times, as you are building your personal brand, you will find that it is going to be a smaller endeavor. Many of those who are trying to build up a personal brand are going to start out basically. If you are just making a personal brand so that you become more employable in an industry, it is likely that you just have a few social media sites running, and you are keeping it all on a small scale. But if you want to take it to the next level and have a big personal brand, like what we see with the celebrities and some other well-known people, then you are going to need to bump up your social media presence.

When you start, it is your job to maintain the social media accounts. And it is probably a good idea for you to be the one to maintain them for as long as possible. You can consider having a team around who will be able to advice you of the best way to keep that account going, when to post, and to look over the analytics with you.

But these social media accounts are meant to be your own personal voice. You are supposed to show more about your products, share information that you think that others in your target audience are going to enjoy, and really showcase your own hobbies, interests, and more on there as well. This needs to be a nice personal touch. You can have your team do all that they want with the other parts of your brand, but for the most part, your target audience still expects that you are going to be the one who runs your own social media accounts.

The second that you start letting someone else do this, it is going to cause some issues with your brand. You will start to lose some of your own voice. You may find that the other person, even if they have a lot of experience behind them, just doesn't get the voice that you are trying to portray here. And you may find that you are going to miss the mark with your consumer.

Since social media is going to be a huge way that you meet up with and interact with your target audience, this is not a place that you want to leave to chance or have mess up for you. Doing the work on your own, even if you have to go through and make some of the posts on your own ahead of time and schedule them for yourself, can make a big difference in the interaction and the connection that you will make with your consumer.

Strategy planning

In the beginning, you are going to be the one who needs to get in there and create the winning strategy that you will use. You need to have an idea about the social media sites that you will post on, the target audience you would like to work with, and all of the other factors that you are going to work with. In the beginning, it is likely that you will keep it pretty small, working with just one or two social media accounts, and maybe a blog to make this easier to manage.

Hopefully, if you are successful, your brand is going to start growing. And as you see it grow, the strategy is going to be much harder for you to manage on your own. This is when you may want to consider working with a strategy planning team. They will have a lot more resources than you to figure out what is working on your brand, and what you may need to change.

This doesn't mean that you need to completely get yourself out of the picture. But it does mean that you need to consider whether you are able to handle all of the work on your own or not. Working with a strategy planning team will ensure that you can grow more, that you can be on as many social media sites as you would like and still see results, and that your message, no matter where you send it out, is still going to be seen by the people who matter the most.

Once you have this team in place, make sure that you all come together and check that you are on the same page. You want to have regular meetings, even if it is just one or two people on the team, about what you want your message to say, where you want to post, if there are going to be any big events that are going to happen with your brand, and anything else that could be important for this process.

Other

There are a lot of people you can work with when it comes to ensuring that you are going to get the best out of your personal branding. This is not something that is going to happen overnight, and it can actually take quite a bit of time for you to see the results. Having a good team on your side to help you understand what needs to be done, to keep you on track, and to keep all of the plates spinning at the same time can be one of the greatest things that you do for your personal brand.

SOCIAL MEDIA MARKETING AND PERSONAL BRANDING

Depending on the type of personal branding that you are trying to do, it is possible that you will need a few other people on your side to ensure that you can get it all done. The number of people, and the job that they will have will all depend on what you are trying to do. If you decide to publish some workout videos, you may need to have a few people on your team to workout with you. If you are cooking, you may need some people to look up recipes, shop, and prepare the food for you.

This is where you really need to have a good strategy in place to help you get started with your personal branding. You need to make sure that you are able to pick out the right team to help you get the work done. You don't want to hire people for jobs that don't need to be done, and you don't want to hire too many people when you could, and should, do some of the work on your own. Knowing what your personal brand needs, and what you should have in place to make it work, can help make it more successful.

Creating your own personal brand is going to take a lot of work. It is going to take a lot of work and some time, you will find that having a good team behind you can make your personal brand more successful. You want to take some time to learn more about your brand, and what it will take to get it off the ground and running, and from there you can pick out the team that you really need to see the best results!

Chapter 9: Creating Your Personal Brand on Facebook

One of the first places that you an start on when it is time to create your own personal brand is through Facebook. This is a social media site where billions of people throughout the world have a profile, or use it in different ways. It is likely that a lot of the people you are targeting will spend some time searching for you on here. Being able to create a good personal brand on tis social media site can help you get further in your personal efforts.

When you are using Facebook to grow your personal brand, there are a few things that you need to consider. First, you need to define yourself. Try to figure out what your own personal brand is going to stand for. You should have a pretty good idea of how to do this from the other steps that we have talked about before. But taking some time to plan ahead so that you keep everything together, so that the story is cohesive, and so you are able to get the results that you would like out of this process.

Once you have a good idea of how you would like to define yourself, it is time to go trough and choose your friends carefully. You are trying to build up a brand, and come up with a new network that is nice and strong. You do not want to waste your time inviting anyone and everyone on Facebook to join you. It is important for you to carefully choose who you would like to share your information with, and whom you are "seen" with on this site. Make sure that you spend time interacting with those who your brand is built for. You can include people like future employees, colleagues, your boss, or clients you would like to attract to you.

Now you need to decide on your strategy. Just like a company will do when it is time for them to brand a new product, you need to come up with a good branding strategy as well. While it is possible for you to work on changing this up over time, it is a good idea for you to

SOCIAL MEDIA MARKETING AND PERSONAL BRANDING

write out much of the strategy, and your plans, as possible. Think about where you would like this branding to go, what your branding will get you to in the future, and more. This can help you to know when you should post content, and what should be in the content, to really reach your target audience.

While you are working on creating your content, and getting it all set up, take some time here to change up your privacy settings. If you are serious about creating your own personal brand, then you need to take some time to filter out all of the content and information that you put out there. You have some choices here. You can choose to not let certain people see your profile. You can cut off certain groups, and more. Or, if you want to keep most of it private to the genera audience on Facebook, but you would still like a way to get others to come and look at your page, you can let some of the information be accessible to the public, or some of the ones you are not friends with.

Along these lines, make sure that you don't let out too much of your own personal information here. You want to talk about things that go with your brand, but telling everyone about all your problems, about the fight that you had with your spouse, and more, is going to harm the brand image that you are trying to come up with here. You can talk about things like your educational information, your successes, your work information, and anything that relates back to the personal brand that you want to create.

While you are in the settings, make sure that you turn off any of the tagging options on pictures. This ensures that you are going to be protected from malicious attacks, spam, and other things that could be unpleasant. In some cases, the issue could be with a good friend who didn't care that much about their internet presence, and they post something that could hurt your image or embarrass you. Turning this tagging feature off can help keep your page clear and prevents any of this happening.

Another option to work with is to create your own vanity URL. This is a domain that you can use on Facebook. This is basically going to take away all of those numbers and letters that Facebook automatically gives you and allows you to have a URL that is easier to recognize and use.

Since you are working on your own personal branding here, you will want to take some time to go through and fill in all of the professional details that you can. This is one of the neat things about Facebook because it will allow you to explain more about what you do in y our position, rather than just typing in the position of the company you are in.

This is a great way for you to take things a step further and really explain what you do in your position. You can talk about what your goals are in this position, even if you work as freelancing or are starting your own business, and it will ensure that you are able to differentiate yourself from some of the others out there are the market who may be doing the same thing. If someone else lists out financial advisor, but you have a full description about your duties, that is going to stand out.

Once your profile is all set up and ready to go, it is time to start doing the proper networking. This is meant to help you to increase the number of friends you have, and in return, this ensures that you are going to be seen by more people. You should spend some time engaging with the friends you already have on Facebook, produce and send out quality content on a regular basis, and import your contacts as they start to grow.

Posting is so important when you are working on your own personal brand. You are going to lose out on a lot of followers and friends, and your personal brand is never going to grow if you do not post updates and content on a regular basis. You need to post things that are interesting, things that are going to keep the interest of your friends, and will convince them to keep coming back over and over again.

SOCIAL MEDIA MARKETING AND PERSONAL BRANDING

First, you need to make sure that you are posting on a regular basis. This number is going to be different for each person, and you may find that what works the best for one person isn't going to work for you. Experiment a bit to see what seems to work the best for you. At least once a day is usually best. If you only post sporadically, your friends will have no reason to come back and check out the content that you are providing. But if you post every hour or more, this is just going to get annoying and people will stop as well.

You also have to pay attention to the things that you choose to post. You don't want to post things that have nothing to do with your personal brand, or the things that you want to showcase here. You want to make sure that it fits with your strategy, it fits with your personal brand, and that will catch the attention of your audience. You can post updates, you can post articles about the topic, and other information that helps you to promote the image that you want to your consumer.

The pictures that you post on Facebook can be important as well. While pictures are not as important on Facebook as they are on other social media sites like Pinterest and Instagram, you still can make good use of these in order to get the results that you would like. You should start out by putting up a profile photo that is professional and high quality. The picture that you choose is going to depend on what you are trying to promote. A young professional who is looking for a job is going to post a different picture compared to someone who is trying to do a new show on YouTube and wants to get noticed.

While we are here, make sure that you take special care of all the pictures that you post on your profile. Everything, whether it is the articles, the posts, and the pictures, need to fit in with the strategy that you set up before. You want it to all fit with the image that you are projecting to your potential consumer, and the pictures you choose can definitely do this. You just need to make sure that you are using them in the proper manner.

Next, you should link your Facebook page to some of the other social media pages that you are trying to do. This is going to help you to reach more people, and can raise some more interest in what you do, and in yourself in particular. The more people who visit your blog, or your other social media sites, will find that this cohesion makes you look more professional. If you find that across your social media pages, and anything else that you are using, that something doesn't end up matching together, it is time to work on it, or choose not to link it. You should also consider having the same e-mail or username address for all of the accounts so that you can keep the branding going among more than one account.

Once all of this is set up, it is time to consider running a new group or a new page on Facebook. If you already have quite a few friends on Facebook, you will be able to increase this number with the help of a new page. This is a great way for you to promote your personal brand, along with your interests and your business. When you make a group, you will be able to connect to more people. The people who are interested in the same interests as you, or who are on the same topics as your personal brand, will be able to find this page, and you will get some organic growth to your network and to your brand over time.

Once you are ready, you are able to work with Facebook events. You will be able to make your own event, or you can promote an industry event or gathering in that area. You can even use this kind of event to encourage your current friends and followers to come out and get more of their friends to follow you as well.

Make sure that any event that you choose to do is set up well, and is able to meet the needs that you have. if you are able to make it interesting, and ensure that it stays with the strategy that you already have, while fitting with that new brand that you are trying to grow, it can do some wonders for increasing your reach. It can even make your consumer and friends feel like they are doing something important, or like it is well worth their time in other ways.

SOCIAL MEDIA MARKETING AND PERSONAL BRANDING

There are a lot of different ways that you are able to grow your own personal brand. But one of the first places that you need to look at for doing this, mainly because of all the options and all of the people who are on this social media site, is Facebook. This chapter has the tips and tricks that you can use in order to take that personal brand, and get it to flourish when you use Facebook to help you to do it!

Chapter 10: Creating Your Personal Brand on Instagram

After Facebook, Instagram is a great online platform that can help you to get some of the following that you want for your own personal brand. This is a very popular photo uploading platform where you are able to post and share both images and videos.

As someone who is looking to grow their own personal brand, it is worth your time to look into Instagram. It currently has more than 150 million users, and more than 5 billion pictures uploaded. What this means is that this is a social network that has a very wide range of audience, whether they are real photographers who are using this, or just some of the general users to the whole thing.

But you will find that Instagram is so much more than just a social network that you can use. It has actually become one of the best platforms to use if you want to build up your personal brand. This social media platform has become a big market for individuals and companies alike who want to be able to build up their own personal brands, and it is easy to find a ton of celebrities who have gone on there and started to build up a brand as well.

This social media site is very full of images and videos and more. This means that, even though you are able to write some information with the pictures, you need to concentrate more on the visuals than anything else. The first thing that anyone is going to see is the pictures, and they actually have to go through the process of clicking on the picture before they even see any words. Working on high-quality images to help promote your brand is something that you will need to consider.

If you are interested in working with Instagram to work on your personal brand, you need to make sure that you know how to come up with high quality content. Some of the things that you can consider when it comes to creating your own personal brand on Instagram includes:

Go with a username that is unique

Many new brands on Instagram are not going to take the time to pick out a username that is unique. But since this username can help portray a lot of characteristics about your brand, it is important that you choose it wisely.

First, remember that you should not go with a username that is long and hard to remember. And don't go for one that your followers are not able to pronounce. If your followers aren't able to remember it, they won't. They will just give up and choose not to follow you any longer. With this in mind, you want to make sure that you go with a username that is easy to remember, simple, and easy for your followers to find.

If you plan on using more than one social media site to help promote your brand, it is helpful to use the same unique name for all of the handles. This makes it easier for your followers to find you, no matter what site they are on.

Build a unique persona

One of the big keys tat you will notice when it comes to building up your personal brand is uniqueness. Your exclusivity is going to create a favorable kind of opinion in the minds of others. There are a lot of ways tat you are able to do tis from your profile picture to the information that you present, and even with the postings that you choose to do.

Try to find ways that you can show off your brand, and even your personality, in the posts that you are doing. This is going to help draw more people in, and will make it easier for you to get the results that you want. The more that you are able to set yourself apart form others, and really showcase what makes you so special compared to the rest, the better you will be when it comes to growing that brand.

Working with hashtags

Hashtags are a great ting that you are able to add into your personal branding on Instagram as well. These hashtags are going to make it easier for others to search for you in the community. But for these to work, you need to make sure that you are working with tags that are searched quite a bit, and the ones that are popular. You will find that these hashtags are the smart way for you to reinforce your brand in a way that nothing else can. Users who don't really know much about these hashtags are going to make a story out of using a long list of hashtags, which comes out looking messy, and can turn your followers off.

Picking out the right hashtags can make a big difference in how successful that you will be with people finding your videos and pictures. Make sure that you do your research and find the ones that are going to match what your followers are looking for, and what works the best for your business.

One thing that can really help your brand to grow is to create and then promote your own personal hashtag. When you make your own hashtag, it is going to highlight your brand, and can help make it stronger. You need to come up with something that is unique, something that you know no other business or brand has, and something that will set you apart from the rest of the competition. Make sure that you put this unique tag on all of your promotional items, your pictures, and your videos and try to promote it with your followers.

Post images that are exclusive

You can also consider posting images that are exclusive These can be the ones that have just shown up on the web within a few minutes and you are one of the first to showcase these, or the pictures that you were the one to take. Generally photographers are going to be used in order to get these pictures set up, but if you are trying to build up a new brand on your own, then this is something that you would want to do as well.

No matter what kind of brand you are trying to build up, you should consider working with this idea. You can show exclusive items, pictures, videos and more, especially if you are only showing this information on your Instagram page, rather than on all the other ones as well. You will find that this is a great way to establish the brand that you want, and will help you to gain more followers over time as well.

Working on your profile

Your profile is going to be one of the first things that your follower is going to see when they get on Instagram. You want to make sure that this is going to be set up in a way that you are able to impress them. And, if you are able, you want the follower to know what your brand is all about as well.

When you are working on the information and the picture that is on your profile, you need to pay special attention. You want to choose a picture that is original, and high quality. Or, if you have a logo, you can put this on there as well. You want this picture to tell people what your profile is about. The information that you place on the profile needs to explain about your brand and what it is going to deal with.

With the right information, and some good pictures on the profile, you will find that it is easier for users to recognize your brand, and they will quickly be able to recognize what kind of updates they can expect to find on the page. If you want to, consider adding a bit more information so that your followers, or anyone who is interested in you. This can include your Facebook and Twitter account handles, your phone number, and your professional email address to make things easier.

Be careful with your tagging

Tagging can be something that helps you out a lot with your profile. But you do need to be careful with this. You don't want to just tag everyone you can find, because this means that you are going to tag people who are not supposed to be tagged. If you do decide to tag people, make sure that you are careful with who you place on the picture or the video. Only add them if they have approved, and if it makes the most sense.

Consider doing contests

Another option that a lot of people like to do when they start on Instagram, and when they want to work on their own personal brand, is to run contests. You can choose how often you would like to do this, including each week or each month. These are helpful in order to help you get more visitors to your profile, which can do wonders for how much you are able to grow your brand and become recognizable throughout the world. These contests are going to bring you a lot of results that are pretty impressive, including the ability to boost the productivity of your brand by 80 percent or more.

The way that you do this contest is going to depend on what works the best for you. You may make sure to offer up some prizes to the winners of the contest to entice them to help you out. But if you choose to go with the prize option, make sure that you actually give out the prizes. Many companies have ruined their reputations because they did social media contests and then never announced the winners or gave out the prizes that they had promised.

Tell a story

When someone comes to your profile, they should be able to see a nice story spelled out there. You want your videos and photos to tell the story of your brand. Your followers need to be able to sense this and find it all meaningful. Your users are always looking for something new and interesting so post something that is going to engage the user.

There are a lot of different stories that you are able to make, and it is going to depend on the brand that you are going to portray to others. You always need to make sure that you are impressing those who come to your profile, and that, when they look at the pictures and videos that you post, they will understand what your story is, and more about your brand. If your content is not doing this, then you are wasting a lot of time without building up your brand.

Work on quality

As you are working on your Instagram profile, make sure that you focus on the quality. Many people, especially when they are first getting started, will just focus on the quantity of posts that they are able to post. They don't spend time worrying about how good the quality is, and this is what can hurt them. Any time that you post one image or vide each day, you need to make sure that it meets the excellence that you need before you decide to post it.

You need to be careful with the images that you choose as well. You want the best ones to go with all the posts that you choose. And double check that it is the best one. Remember, all of these are going to portray your image to the outside world. If you post something that is low-quality and doesn't meet up with your brand, it is going to end up harming your personal branding. Make sure that the image and the vide are interesting and carries the ability to enthrall your followers.

Interact with others

One thing that you need to really focus on with your profile on Instagram is to interact with others. It isn't enough to just post a few pictures on the site and hope that others are going to start following you. There are millions of pictures found online, even on Instagram. You need to make sure that you are able to interact with others and make sure that you are forming some relationships with others while you are there.

First, if anyone comments on your pictures or your posts, then you need to try and reply back. This doesn't have to be instant as no one expects you to spend all of your time sitting at the computer and waiting for those comments to come in. Setting aside a bit of time each day to handle these comments and to reply to your followers can make them feel like you truly value them, and will keep them coming back.

You can also work on getting new followers to come to your page and get them to pay attention to you. Finding other pages, especially other personal brands, that you can follow will help. Commenting on pictures that you really like, following the right people, and answering questions, whether they are on your page or on another profile, can really make a difference in your reach, and who decides to follow you.

One note about commenting on other posts and profiles is make sure that they provide some value. Just replying "cool" "yes" "ok" or something similar is not going to work here. That doesn't provide any value. You should add in at least a few sentences to answer questions, and to help you to really provide some value to the others on that page.

Chapter 11: Creating Your Personal Brand on YouTube

YouTube is one of the premier video sharing website in the whole world. While there are thousands of different websites out there that you are able to use in order to try and improve your personal brand, there aren't any that will be able to give you both the reach, and the credibility, that are needed to make a big impact and to get people to notice you like YouTube. But if you would like to create your own personal brand, you need to make sure that you are using YouTube in the right manner. Some of the things that you should keep in mind when it comes to creating a personal brand on YouTube includes

Brand your profile

In order to make sure that you are able to build up a good personal brand on YouTube, you need to consider the best way to position yourself. If you already have a personal brand put in place on some of your other social media sites, then you can simply move it over to your YouTube channel as well. Some of the things that you need to consider when it comes to branding your YouTube channel and getting it all set up and ready to go includes

1. Choose a channel name: Depending on the branding strategy that you choose you use, you can use a unique show name, the name of your company, or even your own full name. Think about the name of your channel carefully as this is going to be the one that you are stuck with for some time.
2. Profile setup: You need to take some time to fill out your profile. This is going to make it easier for others to find you when they do a search. You can also upload an avatar and get that set up so that people can find you even better.
3. Information on the channel Most of those who start to market on their channel don't realize that there are actually a

few account types that they are able to choose. If you consider yourself an expert in the field (or you would like to become one), then you should select the Guru account style. This allows you to come in with a custom logo and makes it easier to add in links.
4. Customizing the channel: When you are ready, you can go and log into the account, and see how the channel is doing. You can then go trough and add in any customizations that you want. You don't want to go crazy with this one, but taking the time to update things and change them around if it meets with your branding can make a big difference.
5. Title and tags on the channel. If you think that there are some good tags that are going to reflect the content of your videos, then go ahead and add them in. Think these ones through because they are going to be critical in helping you to really get others to find your information.
6. Colors and themes In your account, you will be able to take some time to look for the colors and the overall look that will best align with what your brand is all about. Take some time to choose this to ensure it looks nice and cohesive with the rest of the branding that you are doing.

Create some good videos

You do not want to become that person on YouTube who puts up a video that is low quality, the one who just spits them out as quickly as possible in the hopes of getting some more views. There are millions of hours of video on YouTube, so you need to be able to get yourself to stand out from the crowd. And providing your audience with videos that are bad or low quality is going to get you in a lot of trouble.

Content is going to be king, and when you are on YouTube, the only way that you can truly be successful is to make sure that your content is truly worth spreading. This means that it needs to be really interesting or really funny in most cases. In addition to good content, you want to make sure that you have the right kind of equipment to get yourself started. Never put bad or low quality videos on your YouTube channel. You are competing against a lot of other people who are uploading videos and trying to get to the same group as you. If you don't meet the same quality as them, you are going to be the one who loses.

When you are creating videos for your YouTube channel, think about the brand that you want to promote, and what your audience might like to see. You are still catering to the same audience that you did on some of the other social media sites, even if they haven't had time to look for you here yet. You can then use these ideas to start creating some amazing videos that will not only attract your current audience, but will bring in some new consumers as well.

Promote your videos

When it comes to promoting on YouTube, things may seem a little bit scary. With all of that content already found on this channel, you may wonder how you are going to make your video stick out, and how you will make sure that your audience is actually going to see you. Often, the best way to start promoting your channel, and any of the videos that you have on there, is using the network that you already have.

For example, if you have some other social media sites, make sure to post when you have a new video up. If you use any blogging in this process or in your strategy, writing about a new video, and providing a link, can help. Once your own friends and followers see the video, and like and comment on it, it can help raise you up a bit, and it won't be long before others are able to find out about the amazing content that you produce.

You will find that spending some time on your YouTube channel, and making sure that it is high quality and able to handle all of the branding that you plan to do, can do a lot of good for you. Create high quality videos, add in interesting information to your profile, and work hard to promote your videos, and you will find that working with

YouTube can be one of the best ways to help build up your personal branding.

Chapter 12: Creating Your Personal Brand on Twitter

Twitter can be a great platform that you can use in order to promote your personal brand, but you may find that it is a bit trickier compared to some of the other options. You are only given 140 characters to show your message, and to make sure that you are able to really let your voice, and the voice of your brand, show up for others. This can be a challenge, but you will start to get the hang of it as you work on it.

If you have used the Twitter site for some of your own personal needs, you are probably used to some of the things that you need to do in order to get Twitter to work well for you. But when it is time to make this platform work for your own personal branding, things will need to be changed up a little bit. Some of the things that you can do in order to use Twitter to build up a memorable personal brand include:

Follow the leaders

When you first set up the handle that you would like to use on Twitter, it is time to start following some people. You should take some time to follow a few of the leaders on Twitter. It is best if you are able to find some of the leaders who are in your particular field first. This allow you to do some networking, and can give you plenty of chances to comment and ask questions, opening up the door to how many people will see you.

The beauty of using Twitter is that you won't have to go that far in order to discover the best way to be successful with marketing. You will be able to observe the professionals and see how they do it. You also want to take the time to follow anyone who is sharing a lot of content, and who seems to be on Twitter, and very popular on there.

Over time, in addition to observing some of these accounts and learning how they play the game, it is time to start engaging them. Influencers, just like anyone else, like to hear praise from someone else, so start out with this. Of course, make sure that you don't expect this to turn into a home run. But, if you find that over time, the influencer decides to start following you, or if they even mention you on their page, then this is a big score.

If you do take the time to directly reach out to the other influencer, see what you are able to offer to them in return for them helping you. For example, if part of your personal branding included running a blog, you could offer to mention them in one of your blog posts. This can help them with their reach, while you work on your own reach as well.

Work on the profile and your brand

You do not want to get on any social media sites and not take care of your profile, and make sure that it, and any content that you add to it, are going to work together with your brand. To start, make sure that you go through and work on your profile, just like we have talked about with the other social media platforms on this list. You want to make sure that there is a good picture, one that highlights what your personal brand is all about (please leave the cutesy pet pictures off unless you are a vet or a dogwalker), and fill in all of the information that is there.

Since you are only going to be given 140 characters to go with each post, you do need to be careful about how you are posting things and whether they go along with your own brand or not. You want to still keep the content fresh, and you want to post things that are useful to the audience. Following those influencers above will make it easier for you to really figure out the best way to do this and still get your message across.

Create some good content

If you waste your time tweeting negative things, rather than working on your brand, then it won't be long before you start to build up a negative personal brand on Twitter. You want to make sure that you are tweeting insightful and helpful content so that you are better able to grow your own reputation. There is going to be something in common between all of the Titter brands that are the most impressive and this is that they are gong to post a steady stream of content that is valuable.

One thing to consider is that you can't tweet enough. Of course, this doesn't mean that you should spend every second of every day posting on your profile, and you shouldn't make it your goal to post 100 times a day. but if you see that there is some positive engagement going on with your profile, then it is fine to keep on posting. Unlike some of the other social media sites, Twitter has some more openness when it comes to the number of times you interact and post on there.

The important thing to remember is that the quality that you post needs to be high, and you need to find your own rhythm. If you find that posting every hour, every few hours, or a couple of times a day seems to work for your schedule and for your personal brand, then go ahead and do this. You need to figure out what works the best for you.

Another thing to remember is that you need to come up with some of your own content. It is fine to use some curated content, especially if you feel that it is going to truly benefit your readers. But if you are really serious about getting your own personal brand built up, then you need to post some original content. In fact, the majority of your content needs to be original, or your readers are going to quickly get tired of paying attention to you.

Engaging

Twitter, like some of the other social media sites that you may use, is going to be a two-way street. If you take the time to reach out to others, then it is more likely that they are going to engage wit you. You don't want to just put out some content, whether it is curated or you came up with it yourself, and then hope that the readers are going to do all of the work. You need to be active on the community and do some of the work as well.

You need to make sure that you set aside a bit of time each day to reach out and engage with the tweets of your followers, as well as influencer you would like to build a relationship with. Whether you read through some of the tweets that interest you the most, or you look at a profile, you can then take the time to compliment the other person, ask a question, or do some other things that can form a better connection.

It is best if you are able to handle all of this response on your own. Some beginners think that this is all going to be too overwhelming for them to do on their own, and so they choose to hire this out and do some outsourcing. But all of the most successful Twitter entrepreneurs will agree that it is better to handle the responses on your own, rather than hiring someone else to do it.

Test and analyze

Twitter is a great social media site to work with because it is going to give you feedback that is almost instant. Depending on what you post and who is online, you will see how it performs almost right away. This is why it is such a good place to share a lot of content, especially if you would like to test it out.

Doing this lets you get a good idea of what is resonating the best with your audience, so that you know what works and what doesn't. you can then take this information and bring it to some of the other platforms that you are working with. If you would like to make sure that you can test out your material, and easily find it later, you should use hashtag to make this easier. This is also helpful when you would like to compare how a tweet with a certain hashtag did when it preformed against some of the others that they used as well.

It is always a good thing to test out the information that you are posting online. But with some of the other options that are out there, it can be really hard to know what is going to work until it has been out there for a bit. With Twitter, you are able to get some results in, in a short amount of time.

Decide if you want to outsource

When you are working on Twitter, you don't really need to worry about outsourcing at all. This is really a platform where you should put your own energy and do the work. And since it only takes about 140 characters or less to get the message out there, this isn't something that is going to take up a lot of your time.

When you are working on your own personal brand, and you have a lot of things on your plate to juggle at the same time, it sometimes is tempting to try and find some things that you can do to reduce all the work that you need to do. But with Twitter, as with a lot of the other social media sites that you will work with, it is best if you are able to do the work on your own. This ensures that your voice is maintained, and you get a closer look at your audience to figure out what they really like.

Twitter is a great tool that you can use in order to help build up your own personal brand, especially if you are working with a few of the other social media platforms as well. When you are ready to start adding Twitter to your toolbelt, make sure to check out some of the steps and tricks that you can use to be successful with this above.

Chapter 13: Your Personal Brand Over Time – Tips to Getting the Most Out of Your Personal Brand!

Now that we have spent some time working on personal branding and some of the things that you are able to do with this branding, it is time to take it to the next level. Remember, this personal branding is going to be something that is going to take some time, and a lot of effort to accomplish. but the results are going to be so worth it. When you are ready to start building up your own personal brand, and you are excited to see some of the best results with this, some of the tips that you can follow will include:

Be authentic

When it comes to branding yourself, being authentic is going to be one of the best things that you can do. But what does this really mean? As we mentioned earlier, it means that you need to be yourself. Everyone's got their own quirk. Being able to show this to the people who are watching you, and laughing right along with them when you do something funny or make a mistake, can be a great way to connect with your audience, and to keep them coming back for some more.

Blogging

We have not really had much of a chance to talk about this one in this guidebook yet, though we have mentioned blogs a few times. One of the best things that you can do when you are trying to build up your own personal brand is start a blog. This gets your information out there, allows you to share information with others that they will find interesting, and you can even turn it into a way to make money!

Blogging when you first start out can be a challenge. There are a lot of blogs, on almost any topic that you can imagine out there. But since most of them are not that interesting, and many people give up after a short time working on them, there is still some room for you to come into the market as well. You just need to have the right kind of dedication, and the right determination, to get into the mix and not give up.

When you want to get started with blogging, you need to think about a niche or a topic that you would like to write about, and one that will go with your personal brand. And then you need to get to writing. Make sure that your articles are the right length, usually at least 500 words, though going close to 1000 is often better because it provides you with more room to write out the information that you want to share.

You have to keep a few things in line when writing for a blog. First, you need to take the time to write on a regular basis. In the beginning, writing a post every day is maybe best, so that you can fill up the blog and get content on there right away. But after you have had some time to get some good articles on there, you can back off a bit. Be consistent though. Decide what schedule is best for you, and for your time, and then stick with it. Many people find that writing an article once a week seems to be the best.

The articles that you write on the blog need to be interesting, they need to all go together, and they need to be about something that your target audience is going to be the most interested in. You also want to add in the right keywords to the mix so that your target audience is able to find the articles and look them up when they need something about that topic.

This blogging can take some time. You need to gain some followers, and it does take time. You won't be able to get a ton of followers over to your blog when there are only five articles for them to look at. Writing on a consistent basis, and placing notifications about the blog on all of your social media pages, can help you to gain more followers the organic way.

After you finally have enough readers, you will be able to increase your personal brand some more. You may find that affiliate marketing is a good way for you to find the followers that you need and sell products. You can sell some of the products that you decide to make. It may take some time to make this happen, but if you are willing to put the time and effort in, it is a great way for you to create a nice personal brand, while being able to earn some money in the process.

Provide value to your audience

When you are able to provide value to your customers, it is going to make a world of difference. There are always going to be a lot of competition that comes with any kind of brand that you are trying to work with. This means that you need to be able to show the consumer why you are able to provide some more value compared to the competition.

Now, you need to take some time to figure out what that means for your brand. You need to figure out how you are able to take your brand, your product, and you, and make it stand out from all that the competition is abe to provide. This can be hard. But the sooner that you are able to figure this out, the easier it will be to get yourself to stand out.

Step out of the spotlight.

This one is going to seem like it is a bit out of the normal, and a bit different than we have been talking about so far, but being in the spotlight all of the time can take a big toil on your life. In addition, people sometimes need to miss you a bit so that they start to realize better how much they need you in their life. You don't want to step out for a long time, but if you leave it behind for a few days, or even a week, you may find that it brings a new level to your brand and is so effective in helping you to grow.

This is such a simple trick to work with, and it is going to benefit so many things in your life. First, you get a nice break. Social media is one of the best ways for you to grow your personal brand and to ensure that you are going to be able to make the money that you want. But sometimes, spending hours on social media a day can get exhausting and can drain you out. Taking the time off like this, even for a few days, can help you recharge, and may help you to understand how you need to make some changes to your strategy.

In addition, stepping out of the spotlight is going to make a big difference in how much your followers are going to stick with you. You don't want to go off for too long. There is so much competition, that if you go off the social media for too long, then someone will come in and take the vacuum that you leave behind, and you will need to start from scratch. But you will find that taking a few days off, or maybe a week, you will start a greater connection between you and your consumers, and this can help build up your brand quite a bit.

Be consistent

If there is one secret that you must stick with when it comes to doing well with your personal brand, it would be consistency. Consistency can mean a lot of things. It is not just about posting on social media each day. it is also about having a unifying brand look and messaging overall. So, how do we make sure that we are keeping with this consistency?

First, take a look at all of your social media profiles. Do they all look different, or the same? Some will tell you that you need to have a lot of variety with your content. But in reality, the more consistent that you are with your posts and your social media, the easier it is to grow your following.

Think of it this way, if you had a favorite pop singer, someone you followed all the time, and then they suddenly released a jazz album, it is likely that you are going to lose interest. This doesn't mean that the jazz isn't good, but it does mean that you preferred the original music that they created. This is the same kind of thing that can happen with personal branding. Your audience is going to fall in love with a specific way that you decide to present your content. But if you decide to start changing your tune, or you don't maintain that consistency between all your social media sites, then your consumer is going to jump ship.

Network

There is no way that you are going to be able to grow that personal brand if you don't take some time to network. You need to make sure that you are creating as many connections as you can, both online and in real life. Without these connections, it is hard to spread out the information about your brand, and the fewer people who are going to learn about you.

It is going to be really hard to brand yourself if you are not taking the time to put yourself out there to meet and interact with other people. There are a lot of ways that you can network to help grow that personal brand, and you need to take advantage of as many of these as you possibly can. You can start up a blog, go to that Meetup event, mingle with others who are at the same conference as you, grab some coffee with someone you have just met, post on social media each day, go to a group at the library, and just find ways to be involved. It doesn't matter if you meet someone new online or in real life, you will find that networking is one of the best investments that you can do for yourself.

Remember, the more chances that you get to interact with other people, the larger your network is going to become. While it is sometimes tempting to stick to a niche focused network, you will quickly find that the smartest thing that you can do is to expand into as many other categories as you can. You will be amazed at the people you can meet, and how their expertise, advice, insight and more can make a difference in your own personal branding as well.

Don't let your nerves or your shyness or anything else get in your way. and never get in the habit of saying that you are too busy to network. We are all busy. And we are all a bit nervous when it comes to meeting new people. But you will find that anyone who has ever been successful with personal branding will get out there and try to network as much as possible. And if you want to be successful, then you need to do the same things as well.

Be an expert in your field

No matter what field you decide to brand yourself in, make it a point to become an expert in that field. People like to listen to, and learn things from those who they consider experts in the field. So if you can find some way to position yourself as this expert, you already are ahead of the game.

Branding yourself can sometimes be hard when you aren't sure what your area of expertise is. every influencer has to find their own niche to work in, and from there, they can grow and become an expert. So, if you are working on selling tools in your online store, you want to make sure that the consumer thinks that you are an expert in carpentry, furniture design, or some other relevant niche that is going to help you to sell those tools.

Maybe you are going to sell car parts. If you do this, then you need to find a way to position yourself as an expert in the automotive industry so that you are able to provide value to that group of people. It doesn't matter what field or niche you are in, you will need to make sure that you become an expert in that niche, so that it is more likely that your customer will listen to you.

Another method that you can use that goes along with this is to look at building a brand, personal or otherwise, around the things that you are already an expert in. say that you spend ten years working in a hair salon. You could decide that your personal brand is going to be sharing ways to deal with hair issues while you sell a variety of hair products. You can do this with anything that you want, and it is a great way to show others that you really know what you are talking about, so they are more likely to purchase from you.

Amplify yourself

While we did talk a bit before about why it is so important to be yourself, and to be authentic, amplifying yourself is going to be like the second step to getting this done. In a world, especially online, where there is a lot of noise, it is hard for you to get yourself to stand out from the crowd. When you take the time to amplify yourself, you are going to take the essence of who you are, and then run wild with it.

Keep in mind that for this to work, you need to make sure that you are still authentic. You are not lying about yourself to impress others.

But you are taking what is special and unique about yourself, and then shouting it out to the world, so that they are more likely to hear you and take notice.

For example, if you like to be a big risk taker, you may decide to build up a nice personal brand about how you love to take risks. One idea to do with this is to create some content that shows you doing a ton of activities that are risky, and show you as a kind of daredevil.

In this case, you aren't just talking about how you are a dare devil, and you aren't asking others to take your word for it. But you are amplifying it by quite a bit and showing others how you went about and did all of this as well. This ensures that you are able to sell your product, and really showcase the things that you have in your personal brand. There isn't any lying in here. But you are making sure that others know the true you, and that it stands out in the crowd.

There are a lot of different ways that you are able to amplify yourself, and ensure that you are able to stand out from the crowd. It is all going to depend on the products you are trying to sell, or what you are trying to do with your personal branding strategy. But the trick here is to stand out, to make some noise, and to get others to notice you, without having to lie about yourself and look like you are a fake in the process. This is a fine line, but a sign of a truly effective and successful personal brander is able to stick with this.

As you can see, there are a lot of different things that you can do to make sure that your personal brand is able to grow. Standing out from the crowd is going to be one of the hardest parts of the whole thing. But if you are able to follow the tips above, you are going to see some great results in the process as well.

Thank for making it through to the end of *Personal Branding*, let's hope it was informative and able to provide you with all of the tools you need to achieve your goals whatever they may be.

The next step is to start your own personal brand today. You can work on creating some of the goals that you would like to meet, picking out the type of personal branding that you would like to work with, and even choose your niche. From there you can expand out to find a good mentor, figure out your audience, create a good team, and post up a lot of good content.

As we have discussed in this guidebook, it does take some effort and some time to make all of this happen. You do need to have the right kind of dedication to the cause before you can stand a chance of actually seeing the results that you would like with it. For those who think that they will be able to create their own personal brand in a few weeks, only doing a bit of work on the side, failure is going to come quickly.

But for those who are willing to seriously follow the tips and techniques that we talk about in tis guidebook, you will find that it is easier than you think to make your own personal brand, and to help yourself to stand out. In our modern world, there is a lot of competition to be heard online, but only a few are truly successful and able to make this work!

There are so many reasons why you would want to create your own personal brand. But no matter which method you are picking from, you still need to put in the hard work to make it into a reality. This guidebook took some time to explore how to create your own personal brand through setting goals, picking out a target audience, having a mentor to help walk you through it all, and how a good team can make all the difference

Once you have all of the things above assembled and ready to go, we moved on to some of the ways that you can start and grow your own personal brand. We focused on some of the main social media sites, including YouTube, Twitter, Facebook, and more, so that you can get a good idea of what is expected to get that personal branding started. Of course, you may not be able to put all your energy into each one of these, and may need to choose just one or two for your needs. And that is fine. As you read through this guidebook, you will quickly see (if you know your audience well) which one is going to be the best for you and for your personal brand.

Creating a personal brand can take some time, and you need to be willing to get in there and do the work that is required. You face a lot of competition, but if you are successful, the rewards are going to be so worth it. When you are ready to get started with your own personal branding, and you are ready to see what a difference it can make for you, check out this guidebook to help you get started!

Finally, if you found this book useful in any way, a review on Amazon is always appreciated!

© Copyright - All rights reserved.

The contents of this book may not be reproduced, duplicated or transmitted without direct written permission from the author.

Under no circumstances will any legal responsibility or blame be held against the publisher for any reparation, damages, or monetary loss due to the information herein, either directly or indirectly.

Legal Notice:

You cannot amend, distribute, sell, use, quote or paraphrase any part of the content within this book without the consent of the author.

Disclaimer Notice:

Please note the information contained within this document is for educational and entertainment purposes only. No warranties of any kind are expressed or implied. Readers acknowledge that the author is not engaging in the rendering of legal, financial, medical or professional advice. Please consult a licensed professional before attempting any techniques outlined in this book.

By reading this document, the reader agrees that under no circumstances are the author responsible for any losses, direct or indirect, which are incurred as a result of the use of information contained within this document, including, but not limited to, —errors, omissions, or inaccuracies.

[1] Prices are as of January 2019 and may be subject to change.

[2] Prices are as of January 2019 and are subject to change.

www.ingramcontent.com/pod-product-compliance
Lightning Source LLC
LaVergne TN
LVHW010325070526
838199LV00065B/5659